The Letter To The Hebrews

A Commentary

Dr A. T. Bradford

With Rev Eric Delve

NASB Scripture quotations taken from the New American Standard Bible®, Copyright © 1960, 1962, 1963, 1968, 1971, 1972, 1973, 1975, 1977, 1995 by The Lockman Foundation. Used by permission.

ANIV and NIV Scripture quotations taken from the Holy Bible, New International Version ®. Copyright © 1973, 1978, 1984 Biblica. Used by permission of Zondervan. All rights reserved.

Copyright © 2012 Dr A T Bradford

All rights reserved. No parts of this publication may be reproduced, stored in a retrieval system, or transmitted in any form or by any means, without the prior written permission of the publisher.

Thanks are due to my sons Michael and Stephen, and as always, to my wife Gloria.

Published by Templehouse Publishing, London, England.

www.templehouse-publishing.com

ISBN 978-0-9564798-5-3

Dr Bradford may be contacted via email at info@templehouse-publishing.com

The Letter To The Hebrews

Contents

Introduction	4
Chapter 1	6
Chapter 2	19
Chapter 3	28
Chapter 4	38
Chapter 5	46
Chapter 6	52
Chapter 7	61
Chapter 8	70
Chapter 9	77
Chapter 10	94
Chapter 11	110
Chapter 12	129
Chapter 13	141
Who Wrote Hebrews And When?	152
References	156

The Letter To The Hebrews

Introduction

This book is an attempt to put a Jewish-Christian perspective on a letter written by a Jew to Jews, to encourage them to hold onto the fledgling Messianic-Jewish faith. The believers dispersed by persecution from their fellow Jews in the reaction typified by scholars such as Saul, the disciple of the rabbinic scholar Gamaliel, were under constant temptation to renounce faith in Y'shua's sacrifice and return to the fold of mainstream Judaism. Saul had breathed 'threats and murder against the disciples of the Lord' (Acts 9:1), but persecution also came in subtler, though just as effective means. Ostracism by one's own community was no light matter in a society that offered few other means of social support.

Like the majority of the New Testament, this book appears to have been written prior to the destruction of Jerusalem and its magnificent Temple in AD 70. One of the wonders of the world, this awesome construction of Herod the Great afforded the Jewish people great pride in their faith and their status as the nation chosen by Yahweh through which to demonstrate the munificence of Torah. The book of Hebrews depicts the Jewish priests still at their work of making the daily sacrifices and offerings that the Law directed (Hebrews 10:11), hence the Temple destruction under the oversight of the Roman General Vespasian, culminating with the erasure of all but part of the outer 'Wailing Wall' of the Court of the Gentiles, had yet to occur.

The question of authorship is a disputed one and will be dealt with at the end of this book to avoid distraction from what is unquestionably a masterpiece of Messianic truth.

This is a book that nearly evaded being written. My thanks go to Robert Milne for the seed of motivation, to my co-contributor Rev Eric Delve and most especially to our heavenly Father for continuing to speak afresh through the Book of Hebrews. I hope that the insights gained will benefit the reader to the extent that they will wonder anew at the miracle that is the incarnation and sacrificial death of God's unique Son, Y'shua the Messiah.

Chapter 1

The overarching supremacy of the Son of God, above prophet, Torah and angels

1:1 'God, after he spoke long ago to the fathers in the prophets in many portions and in many ways'

The God of Israel is a God who speaks. There is nothing of the 'dumb idols' that the Apostle Paul reminded the Gentiles in the church at Corinth that they had left behind when they had turned to Christ (1 Corinthians 12:2). [i] The Book of Genesis reveals a Creator whose spoken word brings things into being out of nothing. In the Old Covenant, men and women anointed of God 'spoke' (as in 'proclaimed') his word to his chosen people, directing, consoling, admonishing, rebuking and pointing across time to the coming of the Messiah. God's word came in 'many portions' (KJV: 'at sundry times'). The Greek here is '***polumerôs***', from '***meros***', a 'part of the whole that has been assigned to someone'. [1] The thought here is similar to that contained within the Lord's Prayer - 'Give us today our daily bread' - that resource which we need to be going on with in doing the will of God today. God gives us what we need today for today, and it is his word spoken to us in the present moment that ignites in us the faith and power that we need to serve him in the here and now.

'Many ways' is '***polutropôs***', from '***tropos***' meaning 'manner' in the sense of 'manner of living', or 'way of life'. [2] God's word is given to us to 'keep us in all our ways' and our way of life is intended to reflect Kingdom values throughout. Proverbs 3:5-6 reads: 'Trust in

---

[i] 1 Corinthians 12:2 'You know that when you were pagans, you were led astray to the mute idols, however you were led.'

the Lord with all your heart, and do not lean on your own understanding. In all your ways acknowledge him, and he will make your paths straight.'

'Ways' here in the Hebrew is '***derek***', meaning 'journey' or 'manner', standing metaphorically for life's journey, for which trust in God is needed. The disposition of faith (being trust put into action) leans fully on God and not on the gifts or abilities that God has given. His word to us each day for our individual points of need is what provides the faith in us through which God is pleased to move. A single word from Jesus, 'Come', was sufficient to generate in Peter the faith and power needed to propel him out of a boat onto a storm-tossed Lake Galilee. Matthew 14:29: 'He said, "Come!" And Peter got out of the boat, and walked on the water and came toward Jesus.' Faith generated in Peter the power to act on the seemingly impossible word of command spoken to him.

God's prophets had spoken to the Fathers of Israel concerning the coming of the Messiah. Unfortunately most were not sufficiently in touch with God to recognise Messiah when he arrived. Gentile Magi and religiously unclean shepherds responded instead. The idea that Messiah would be revealed to the Gentiles before the wider people of Israel would have been quite extraordinary to Jews. Even Jewish shepherds were despised by the religious authorities (the Mishnah lists them as being unsuitable to give evidence, [3] and their work regularly exposed them to animal sources of uncleanness). But God chose to speak to them of the birth of Messiah, and his word, preserved in the original languages of the Scripture, is still being fulfilled today. The same God is still speaking to us. Whether or not we hear him and respond to him is dependent on the attitude of our hearts. Sadly, the attitude of the religious leaders of Jesus' day excluded them from recognising him at the point at which he was being revealed to the world.

1:2 'In these last days has spoken to us in his Son, whom he appointed heir of all things, through whom also he made the world.'

There has been no clearer word from God, nor could there ever be, than the one made visible in the person of the Lord Jesus Christ in whom, as Colossians 2:9 states, 'Dwells all God's fullness in bodily form'. As Jesus said, 'He who has seen me has seen the Father' (John 14:9). The person of Jesus is the very bodily form of the triune God, limited only in the sense of being in one place at one time and fully dependent on his Father. As such he is a model example of what sonship is supposed to look like, for human men and women to follow. Everything God made was through and for his beloved Son, [ii] who is pleased to share them with those whom the Father adopts back into the dignity of his spiritual family. Jesus' disciple John records (1:3), 'In the beginning was the Word, and the Word was with God, and the Word was God. He was in the beginning with God. All things came into being through him, and apart from him nothing came into being that has come into being.' Jesus played an integral part in the creation of matter both visible and invisible.

Jesus is the 'Word of God', the 'Word become flesh' (John 1:14), in order that we might see with human eyes what God is like, and it was this person of the creative Word that was in action with God the Father at the point of creation ('In the beginning'). Proverbs (8:27-31, NIV) speaks of Jesus' role in the creation, as wisdom personified. 'I was there when he set the heavens in place, when he marked out the horizon on the face of the deep, when he established the clouds above and fixed securely the fountains of the deep, when he gave the sea its boundary so the waters would not overstep his command, and

---

[ii] Romans 11:36 'For from him and through him and to him are all things.'

when he marked out the foundations of the earth. Then I was the craftsman at his side. I was filled with delight day after day, rejoicing always in his presence, rejoicing in his whole world and delighting in mankind.' The word for 'craftsman' here is '***amon***', which also means 'master workman' or 'architect'. The Greek equivalent is '***architekton***', the word that the Apostle Paul (a tentmaker) [4] used to define his own ministry. Jesus' adoptive father (Joseph ben Heli) was a '***tekton***', hence Jesus' work with his architect father Joseph exactly parallels his role in creation alongside his heavenly Father. [5]

Paul records (Colossians 1:16) that 'By him (*Jesus*) all things were created, both in the heavens and on earth, visible and invisible, whether thrones or dominions or rulers or authorities, all things have been created through him and for him.' Jesus is therefore 'heir to all things' and invites all the adopted children of God to share with him in his inheritance (Romans 8:17 - suffering may be involved). Jesus knows what it is like to be an adopted child; Joseph legally adopted him rather than give Mary up to a charge of unfaithfulness during betrothal (a capital offence under the Oral Law that governed their society).

1:3 'And he is the radiance of his glory and the exact representation of his nature, and upholds all things by the word of his power. When he had made purification of sins, he sat down at the right hand of the Majesty on high.'

Jesus' radiance was revealed to Peter, James and John on the Mount of Transfiguration. Mark 9:3 reads, 'His raiment became shining, exceeding white as snow; so as no fuller on earth can whiten them' (KJV). It was revealed again to John in exile on the Isle of Patmos. 'His head and his hairs were white like wool, as white as snow; and his eyes were as a flame of fire; and his feet like unto fine brass, as if they burned in a furnace; ... and his countenance was as the sun shineth in his strength' (Revelation 1:14-16, KJV). All the fullness of God (and that is a lot of 'fullness'!) dwells perfectly in Jesus bodily. Occasionally the disciples were privileged enough to see past the veil of his human flesh to the divinity that lay within. Their response was to fall like dead men. John would write (John 1:14): 'We saw his glory, glory as of the only begotten from the Father, full of grace and truth.' John was never the same again. The riches of God's glory reside in Jesus Christ (Philippians 4:19), and he promises to share this with us, though, once again, some suffering may be involved (1 Peter 5:10).

Created matter consists of electronic particles that naturally repel each other; the power of Jesus' spoken (*'rhema'*) word holds everything together. [iii] God's word contains power in and of itself, power to create something from nothing out of his own nature and being, as in the creation of the world. The reverse is also true - one day the heavens and earth that we know will be released to 'roll up like a scroll' (Isaiah 34:4, Revelation 6:14), and new ones made in their place for God's adopted children to live in.

Jesus came to 'make purification for sins'. Sin robs mankind of participating in God's promises, causing us to be 'without a share' in them, because by 'missing the mark' we fall short of God's standards. The Greek word for 'sin' used here (*'hamartia'*) carries both of these meanings. This is distinct from the word used in the Lord's Prayer (*'opheilêma'*), which means 'a debt' (in that instance of a moral nature). 'Purification' is *'katharos'*, from which we derive the English word 'cathartic', expressing a purging and expulsion in an ongoing way of all that defiles. The reference applies to the action performed by the High Priest who made purification for the people of Israel in the Holy of Holies once a year on the Day of Atonement. Of the High Priest the Book of Leviticus records: 'When he goes in to

---

[iii] Colossians 1:17 'He is before all things, and in him all things hold together.'

make atonement in the holy place, no one shall be in the tent of meeting until he comes out, that he may make atonement for himself and for his household and for all the assembly of Israel. Then he shall go out to the altar that is before the Lord and make atonement for it, and shall take some of the blood of the bull and of the blood of the goat and put it on the horns of the altar on all sides. With his finger he shall sprinkle some of the blood on it seven times and cleanse it, and from the impurities of the sons of Israel consecrate it' (Leviticus 16:17-19). Hebrews 9:12 records that Jesus entered the Holy of Holies in heaven (of which the tabernacle and temple were copies) with his own blood, to offer it there before his Father for our sins and so make a once-and-for-all offering of atonement (an exchange that brings a reconciliation towards favour and acceptance). Having completed his mission of salvation he then sat down at his Father's right side, symbolic of the equality of shared authority.

After the Lord Jesus had spoken his last words to his disciples, Mark (16:19), records that Jesus 'was received up into heaven and sat down at the right hand of God'. From this shared authority comes the 'great commission' of Matthew 28:18-19, 'All authority has been given to me in heaven and on earth. Go therefore and make disciples of all the nations.' To be at someone's 'right hand' is synonymous with sharing in exercising their authority.

1:4 'Having become as much better than the angels, as he has inherited a more excellent name than they.'

The writer to the Hebrews favours using the word 'better' to ascribe to Jesus, he uses it 12 times. It is **'*kreittôn*'**, meaning 'excellence', from **'*kratos*'**, meaning 'strength in authority or dominion'. Hence it is linked to the right to rule. Jesus as the second member of the Triune Godhead has a right to rule that is unsurpassed by any created being, whatever their angelic rank may be.

Jewish society was divided as to the place and role of angels. Whereas the Sadducees did not believe in them, the scholars did, a fact that the Apostle Paul used to his advantage whilst on trial before the Sanhedrin. 'The Sadducees say that there is no resurrection, nor an angel, nor a spirit, but the Pharisees acknowledge them all" (Acts 23:8). The even stricter Jewish sect of the Essenes likewise believed in them. Josephus notes: 'He swears to communicate their doctrines to no one any other way than as he received them himself; that he will abstain from robbery, and will equally preserve the books belonging to their sect, and the names of the angels' (Josephus' 'The Wars of the Jews' Book 2, Chapter 8).

Angels were believed to have been attendant at the giving of the Law to Moses on Mount Sinai. This was based on rabbinic interpretation of Moses' words in Deuteronomy 33:2. "The Lord came from Sinai, and dawned on them from Seir. He shone forth from Mount Paran, and he came from the midst of ten thousand *holy ones*; at his right hand there was flashing lightning for them." 'Holy ones' is '**qadosh**', meaning 'set apart', and was rendered as 'angels' in the Septuagint (the Greek version of the Hebrew Old Testament). The first martyr Stephen addressed the Sanhedrin along these lines: "You who received the law as ordained by angels, and yet did not keep it" (Acts 7:53). And so the writer to the Hebrews begins his letter by introducing Jesus as being incomparably greater to any of the previous ways in which God had 'spoken' (verse 1), greater than any prophet and greater than the giving of the Law or any of the angels that attended it being given.

The concept of Jesus being made 'a little lower than the angels' (Psalm 8:5 and Hebrews 2:7) can cause some confusion in regard to Jesus' status in his human (incarnate) form. The Hebrew word for 'lower' in Psalm 8 ('**chaser**') means to decrease and become empty, which Jesus did in taking on the role of servanthood. Philippians (2:6-8) records that 'Although he existed in the form of God, he did not regard equality with God a thing to be grasped, but emptied himself, taking the form of a bond-servant, and being made in the likeness of men. Being found in appearance as a man, he humbled himself by becoming obedient to the point of death, even death on a cross.' The equivalent Greek word used in Hebrews is '*elattoô*', meaning to be lower in dignity. The idea of God becoming man with the attendant indignities of all the natural bodily functions of the renal and digestive tracts, etc., must surely have been mind-boggling to the watching angels, not to mention the indignities associated with the crucifixion. Such is the sacred nature of the love of God; no price was too great to pay to restore fallen men and women to right relationship with him.

Vine's Expository Dictionary defines the 'name' that Jesus received as part of his inheritance and reward for his sacrifices as describing his 'authority, character, rank, majesty, power, excellence, etc.; of everything that the 'name' covers'. Jesus' 'name', in terms of his fame and reputation is rightly far above all other 'names' (Philippians 2:9). [iv] Angels can only stand in awe and wonder, and so should we.

1:5 'For to which of the angels did God ever say, "You are my Son; today I have begotten you." And again, "I will be a Father to him, and he shall be a Son to me?"'

The first rhetorical question from Psalm 22:7 is answered with an emphatic negative. The second is from God's word via Nathan to David in regard to Solomon (2 Samuel 7:14) which the writer extends to apply to David's greater descendant Jesus. No angel enjoys a relationship with the Almighty God as their Father, one reason that man can be described as 'a little less than God' (Psalm

---

[iv] 'God highly exalted him, and bestowed on him the name which is above every name' (Philippians 2:9).

8:5 - '*Elohim*' here means 'God', not 'angels'). This is why God's adopted children shall judge angels (1 Corinthians 6:3). As joint-heirs with Christ (Romans 8:17) we have a far greater authority than angels have. If only we were better placed to utilise it! By holding fast to God's promises and resisting the devil's accusations we can stand and exercise godly authority over what we are responsible for.

The concept of being 'begotten' has sometimes been assailed by those (such as Jehovah's Witnesses) who seek to depict Christ as a created spirit-being rather than as the person of God himself. The Greek word here is '***gennaô***', meaning to 'begat' and used commonly in Scripture to describe a father who has had born to him a son who will inherit from the father and who shares the father's name and identity. The distinction is therefore between one's own flesh and blood as compared to what one has fashioned with one's own hands, similar to the distinction between a potter's first-born son and a piece of pottery that the potter has made. This family-type relationship is what characterises the triunity of God and is also supposed to characterise God's people, fashioned after God's own image and growing towards the fullness of maturity so splendidly modelled by Jesus himself on earth.

1:6 'And again, when he brings the firstborn into the world, he says, "And let all the angels of God worship him."'

The term 'firstborn' has two meanings. It can mean the first child (usually the first male child in biblical times) born to someone, or it can have the more particular meaning of the status and position in relation to the father ascribed to such a child. In Hebrew thinking, the firstborn had a special place and special responsibilities to the family, for example in relation to marriage (Genesis 29:26), blessing (Genesis 48:18), sanctification (Exodus 13:2 and Numbers 3:13) and also in receiving a double portion of the father's inheritance

(Deuteronomy 21:17). The nation of Israel is God's firstborn of the nations (Exodus 4:22). Jesus too holds the title of 'firstborn' (Colossians 1:14 - 'The image of the invisible God, the firstborn of every creature') in the sense of the authority and privileges that come from being 'over all of creation', and not in the sense of being created. On the contrary, Colossians (1:1) makes it clear that Jesus was integral to the creation of all things. 'For by him were all things created, that are in heaven and that are in earth, visible and invisible, whether they be thrones or dominions or principalities or powers: all things were created by him, and for him' (KJV). As 'firstborn', Jesus came 'from the dead' in resurrection glory; death had no power over him. The song of Moses (Deuteronomy 32:43) records in the Septuagint, 'Make his people rejoice, oh nations, and let all the angels worship him.' This was sung at the point when the firstborn nation of Israel was birthed into freedom from slavery to the Egyptians through the parting of the Red Sea, and the subsequent drowning of the pursuing Egyptian army, prompting worship of the God who had delivered them from Egypt. This is a prophetic forerunner of the worship that occurred when God brought his firstborn Son into the world from the womb of his virgin mother Mary. 'Suddenly there was with the angel a multitude of the heavenly host praising God, and saying, "Glory to God in the highest, and on earth peace, good will toward men"' (Luke 2:13-14, KJV).

1:7 'And of the angels he says, "Who makes his angels winds, and his ministers a flame of fire."'

'Winds' here is '*pneuma*', meaning 'spirit'; angels are spirit-beings that were created before the creation of the world. Revelation (12:4) indicates that one-third of them joined Satan in his exercise of his freewill in rebelling against their creator and becoming demons. Even though Jesus' power and authority as the second person of the Trinity far overshadows the angels, they have power to act on God's behalf and manifest his glory (e.g. Daniel 10:6), and such was their appearance that even someone as experienced in the things of God as the Apostle John felt he should worship one (Revelation 19:10). The writer quotes from Psalm 104:4; 'Flame of fire' can also mean 'a lightning strike'; a good illustration of angelic power to act in God's service and under his authority. Angels minister the '***rhema***' word of God, which is itself referred to as a fire. "Is not my word like fire?" declares the Lord, "and like a hammer which shatters a rock?" (Jeremiah 23:29). The verse is also reminiscent of the Jewish wisdom book 2 Esdras (8:20-22) which reads, 'O Lord, thou that dwellest in everlastingness which beholdest from above things in the heaven and in the air; whose throne is inestimable; whose glory may not be comprehended; before whom the hosts of angels stand with trembling, whose service is conversant in wind and fire' (KJV, Apocrypha).

1:8-9 'But of the Son he says, "Your throne, O God, is forever and ever: and the righteous sceptre is the sceptre of his kingdom. You have loved righteousness, and hated lawlessness; therefore God, your God, has anointed you with the oil of gladness above your companions."'

This is a direct quotation from Psalm 45:6-7, a Psalm recognised as messianic by both Jewish and Christian scholars. Verse 8 of Psalm 45 clearly describes the king's robes in ways identical with Jesus' burial cloths ('myrrh and aloes'), and inconsistent with any earthly king (crushed aloes carries a pungent scent which blocks the olfactory nerve's recognition of the smell of decay - a type of first-century air-freshener). Jesus' rule and reign (his 'throne') is eternal; he rules in perfect justice, embodied by the 'righteous sceptre'. He loves what is 'right' - his Father's word, and rejects with strong aversion ('hates') all that seek to oppose it. 'Gladness' is '***agalliasis***', meaning 'exceeding joy', of the type that caused the infant John the Baptist to dance within the womb of Elizabeth at the coming of Mary, who was carrying in her womb the infant Jesus. Jewish festivals were marked with a perfumed anointing of the celebrants; Christ's anointing exceeds all others, just as his mediation between God and man far exceeds that of any angelic being.

1:10-12 'And you Lord, in the beginning, laid the foundation of the earth; and the heavens are the works of your hands, they will perish, but you remain; and they all will become old like a garment, and like a mantle you will roll them up, like a garment they will also be changed, but you are the same, and your years will not come to an end.'

The writer now turns to another Psalm (102:25-27), contrasting God's unchanging nature with the temporal nature of the earth that he has made. One day all that we see will be rolled up (Revelation 6:14) and replaced by an eternal 'new heaven and new earth in which righteousness dwells' (2 Peter 3:13). The English word 'world' is in fact derived from a contraction of 'wear old'. When man has finished spoiling the earth that God made, the eternal and unchanging God will make another and populate it with his adopted children in an eternal heavenly kingdom.

1:13-14 'But to which of the angels has he ever said, "Sit at my right hand, until I make your enemies a footstool for your feet?" Are they not all ministering spirits, sent out to render service for the sake of those who will inherit salvation?'

Psalm 110 is now cited as another messianic Psalm, quoted by Jesus himself as evidence of the divinity not afforded to David but rather to 'his Lord'. Psalms 110:1-2: 'The Lord says to my Lord, "Sit at my right hand until I make your enemies a footstool, for your feet." The Lord will stretch forth your strong sceptre from Zion, saying, "Rule in the midst of your enemies."' As Matthew (22:41-46) records: 'While the Pharisees were gathered together, Jesus asked them,

"What do you think about the Christ? Whose son is he?" "The son of David", they replied. He said to them, "How is it then that David, speaking by the Spirit, calls him 'Lord'? For he says, "The Lord said to my Lord, "Sit at my right hand until I put your enemies under your feet." If then David calls him 'Lord', how can he be his son?" No one could say a word in reply, and from that day on no one dared to ask him any more questions' (NIV). Jesus presents himself as David's Lord. No angel was ever addressed in this way, despite their service toward those that God receives into his family as joint-heirs (Romans 8:17) with his Son, the Lord Jesus Christ.

Through trust in Jesus' sacrifice at Calvary and his subsequent resurrection, men and women receive the amazing privilege of sharing with him his glorious position of ruling at the Father's right hand. God makes 'us alive together with Christ (by grace you have been saved), and raised us up with him, and seated us with him in the heavenly places in Christ Jesus' (Ephesians 2:5-6). We are also afforded the resource and assistance ('***diakonia***' - 'service, ministry') of the angelic beings, in addition to the power of the Holy Spirit who indwells and fills us. Angelic assistance is not presented in Scripture as an ethereal and rather vague form of help. Daniel's intercessions were accompanied by the intervention of the archangel Michael (Daniel 10:13).

The inter-Testamental Jewish wisdom book of Tobit describes the interventions of an angel named Raphael in assisting the righteous Jew Tobit in spiritual warfare (Tobit 8:3). And Jesus himself spoke of angels that can appear before God in heaven on behalf of those they have charge of. "See that you do not despise one of these little ones, for I say to you that their angels in heaven continually see the face of my Father who is in heaven" (Matthew 18:10). The emphasis though is on doing the will of God (often with unrecognised angelic assistance) rather than on focusing upon angels for their own sake.

Chapter 2

'We see Jesus' - his atoning offering that opens the way into the family of God

2:1 'For this reason we must pay much closer attention to what we have heard, so that we do not drift away from it.'

The words of Jesus are of far greater importance than the words of any angel, servants of God though they are. Jesus is the '***logos***', the incarnate word of the Father, and also brings the '***rhema***' (spoken) word of God that ignites faith in us, communicating in pure form the thoughts and intentions of God's own heart for any given moment in time. His words deserve by far the closest attention ('***prosecho***' - 'to pay heed to', which had a nautical connotation, being used of bringing a ship into a dock). [6] The alternative is to let it 'slip away' like running water drifting by - '***pararheo***', from '***rheo***' - 'to flow', a word also with a nautical meaning, used of a ship drifting away. [7] The meaning is that it is easy, particularly with the pressures of modern life, to 'let things slide', but Jesus however deserves our full attention.

2:2-4 'For if the word spoken through angels proved unalterable, and every transgression and disobedience received a just penalty, how will we escape if we neglect so great a salvation? After it was at the first spoken through the Lord, it was confirmed to us by those who heard, God also testifying with them, both by signs and wonders and by various miracles and by gifts of the Holy Spirit according to his own will.'

When God entrusted his word to angelic messengers, it was no more subject to change than his written word to Moses was. God's holiness demands that sin be penalised; Jesus bore the penalty in his own body on the cross, that we might come alive to him and his righteousness (1 Peter 2:24). The gift of God (grace and new life in Christ) is so great that persistently ignoring it will lead to eternal separation from him, a judgement that Jesus spent a lot of time advising people to avoid. The Apostles had faithfully passed on the good news that they had heard from Christ himself; it was now up to the next generation to correctly represent those words in the life-giving power of the Holy Spirit. Jesus had preached the word with signs following; his apostles did likewise (Mark 16:20). The church has a duty to the world to not settle for anything less. This involves being fully in the will of God, led by the flow of his Holy Spirit under the guidance of his word, both prophetic and written (the latter always taking precedence).

The 'gifts' of the Spirit referred to here are literally his 'distributions' ('*mersimos*'). These include the '*charismata*' ('gifts of grace') of 1 Corinthians 12 and 14 (tongues, prophecy etc.), the five-fold ministry gifts of the '*diakonia*' (the apostles, prophets, evangelists, pastors and teachers of Ephesians 4:11), the '*phanerôsis*' ('manifestations of the Spirit' - 1 Corinthians 12:7) and the '*energêma*' ('effectual outworking and operation of the Spirit'). Together they make up the '*pneumatikos*' - the collective term Paul gives in 1 Corinthians (12:1) for all of the gracious gifts that the Spirit gives to the body of Christ.

2:5-8a 'For he did not subject to angels the world to come, concerning which we are speaking. But one has testified somewhere, saying, "What is man, that you remember him? Or the son of man, that you are concerned about him? You have made him for a little while lower than the angels; you have crowned him with glory and honour, and have appointed him over the works of your hands. You have put all things in subjection under his feet."'

The 'world to come' is heaven, a world ruled by Jesus Christ at the right hand of his Father (Revelation 22:3). The use of 'somewhere' or 'in a certain place' (KJV) should not be taken as indicating that the writer did not know the source of the quotation (which is Psalm 8:4-6). The Greek is '***pou***', indicating a question ('Where?'), a rabbinic device which made the hearer bring to mind the whole of the passage being quoted, and not just the verses mentioned. The writer's Jewish audience would have memorised the Psalms as children and were well aware of its messianic nature. The Psalm's servant has made himself 'lower', yet is also 'crowned with glory and majesty' (verse 5). Jesus himself quoted from this Psalm in relation to his triumphal entry into Jerusalem (Luke 19:40).

As mentioned in chapter 1, Psalm 8 has two renderings, firstly that man has been made a little lower than God (Hebrew: '***Elohim***'). Secondly, (in the Greek rendering in the Septuagint from which the writer quotes) that man, and particularly the Son of Man, Jesus, had been made lower than the angels, with the Greek here indicating that it is lower in terms of dignity. No angel ever underwent the indignities that are part and parcel of the human physiological condition. Jesus' willingness to lower himself to the indignities of daily human existence and especially the crucifixion has led to the Father highly exalting him (Philippians 2:9). When Jesus sits as judge of all humanity everything will be put in subjection to him. Until then the church exists as a type of frontier-fort between two kingdoms; one that it is leaving behind (the kingdom of the world) and one that has not yet fully arrived in a visible sense (the kingdom of our Lord and of his Christ - Revelation 11:15).

2:8b-9 'For in that he put all in subjection under him, he left nothing that is not put under him. But now we do not yet see all things subjected to him. But we do see him who was made for a little while lower than the angels, namely, Jesus, because of the suffering of death crowned with

glory and honour, so that by the grace of God he might taste death for everyone.'

Jesus' rule is over all, but not all as yet acknowledge that rule. 'Subjection' here is '*hupotasso*', meaning that everything has been 'placed under' him in terms of order and authority. One day this will be made fully visible, when he returns in glory to judge the living and the dead. Until then we can content ourselves with gazing upon him. To 'see' Jesus is '*blepo*', meaning 'To perceive by the senses, to feel, to discover by use and know by experience, so as to discern mentally, observe, perceive, discover and understand.' [8] Jesus' substitutionary death at Calvary means that those who have placed their trust in him and his sacrifice for their sins do not need to experience the sense of separation from God normally associated with dying. As Jesus said to the penitent thief, "Today you will be with me in Paradise" (Luke 23:43). Jesus underwent ('tasted') the experience of death on the part of all humanity. We who follow him need have no fear of entering where Jesus has already gone on our behalf. Death has no power over us. As Paul wrote to the Corinthians, when we die 'This mortal shall have put on immortality, then shall be brought to pass the saying that is written, 'Death is swallowed up in victory. O death, where is thy sting? O grave, where is thy victory?'' (1 Corinthians 15:54-55, KJV). The early church knew no fear because they lived in the truth that they had already 'died with Christ', and so 'believe that we shall also live with him' (Romans 6:8).

2:10 'For it was fitting for him, for whom are all things, and through whom are all things, in bringing many sons to glory, to perfect the author of their salvation through sufferings.'

Jesus' willingness to endure suffering to complete the task of paying man's penalty and so satisfy both God's perfect justice and mercy was an act of obedience that the Father rewarded with great glory. As he remarked to the despondent disciples on their way to Emmaus, "Was it not necessary for the Christ to suffer these things and to enter into his glory?" (Luke 24:26). Suffering brought Jesus' mission to its completion in a finished or 'perfected' sense - '*teleioô*' here means 'accomplished' or 'finished', hence Jesus' cry from the cross, 'It is finished' (John 19:30).

Jesus is portrayed as the author or captain of the rescue mission to save mankind from hell. 'Author' here is '*archêgos*', meaning literally the 'chief person to start something and lead it forward'. God not only saves us from sin and death, he shares with us his own nature and likeness (his 'glory'). As Paul put it 'We all, with unveiled face, beholding as in a mirror the glory of the Lord, are being transformed into the same image from glory to glory, just as from the Lord, the Spirit' (2 Corinthians 3:18). This transformation occurs as we gaze and meditate upon Christ. The King James Bible translates Christ's role as the '*archêgos*' ('author') as 'Captain', a term that Luke uses to pertain to Christ in Acts 3:15 and 5:31, where it is often translated as 'Prince'.

2:11-13 'For both he that sanctifies and those who are sanctified are all from one Father, for which reason he is not ashamed to call them brethren, saying, "I will proclaim your name to my brethren, in the midst of the congregation I will sing your praise." And again, "I will put my trust in him." And again, "Behold I and the children whom God has given me."'

The new birth that faith in Jesus brings enables us to enter into the Kingdom of Father God as sons and daughters with a share in the spiritual inheritance that is Jesus' by right. The Son of God therefore has 'many brethren' (quoting Psalm 22:22) among which he is the 'firstborn'. As Paul puts it: 'Those whom he foreknew, he also predestined to become conformed to the image of his Son, so that he would be the firstborn among many brethren' (Romans 8:29). God's existence outside the confines of time (though he chooses to enter it and work in it), means that he has already seen who will and will not choose to respond to his gracious invitation to be born again ('born from above' - John 3:3). He can 'foreknow' this without dictating the choice of someone's own freewill. When we respond to him and join his family through faith in Jesus' sacrifice he repairs the sin-scarred image of him that we bear (having been originally made in his likeness) and re-paints it afresh in the family likeness, causing us to look increasingly like Jesus himself in our natures and characters.

We can join with Jesus in singing his Father's praises as an equal part of the great chorus in heaven's 'congregation', in the midst of the '*ekklesia*', that great 'assembling' of all the citizens of heaven. The quotation 'I will put my trust in him' is found in Isaiah 8:17, as is 'Behold, I and the children whom God has given me' (Isaiah 8:18). 'Trust' is integral both to entering the family of God and also to functioning within it in the family likeness that all God's children share in. We are not supposed to live within the kingdom with a different disposition (e.g. self-reliance) to the one that we gained entry by. 'Trust' here is '*peithô*', meaning 'confidence' (in the Father in this instance), and is the word from which '*pistis*' is derived, being the main New Testament word for 'faith' (active trust).

2:14-15 'Therefore, since the children share in flesh and blood, he himself likewise also partook of the same, that through death he might render powerless him who had the power of death, that is the devil, and might free those who through fear of death were subject to slavery all their lives.'

God the Father's wonderful gift of the Incarnation shows that he was willing to cross the sin-divide and come himself in the person of the second member of the Godhead and clothe himself with human flesh, sharing with us in all its associated limitations and indignities. That person was known on earth as Jesus of Nazareth, the son of Mary and Joseph. The Incarnation is still an extraordinary concept - that God would want to become man would have been an offensive idea to Greeks who held that human flesh corrupted the spirit. It was also not something that the Jews were expecting either, despite the Hebrew Scriptures prophetic allusions to it; rather they anticipated a political deliverer in the manner of Judas Maccabeus, who overthrew the oppressive Greek Seleucid rule in 165 BC.

In 'partaking' ('*koinonia*', meaning 'fellowshipping') in human flesh and blood, Jesus could become food for death, that great scourge of sin-afflicted mankind. When he defeated death through his bodily resurrection three days later, he showed in his new and incorruptible body that death could similarly be overcome by all who would follow in his footsteps. For the believer in Jesus, death is now no more than 'a falling asleep' (as with Stephen's martyrdom - Acts 7:60), a simple point of entry into the real life of eternity, an exit-door from this life into a new and infinitely better eternal one. And so death is robbed of its power to frighten us by our trusting in the love of the One who waits for us, in person, beyond that doorway. The slavery to the Law is ended by our new relationship of sonship-based servanthood of God; the slavery to fear of death is similarly ended by relationship to and trust in him. The absence of the fear of death in the lives of the early believers robbed their earthly rulers of the power to frighten them with the threat of death. Jesus promised the church in Smyrna that those who were faithful to death would receive the crown of life (Revelation 2:10).

The fellowship that exists within the three members of the Godhead, and defines the triune nature of God is extended to all who will receive his gracious invitation to respond in faith and trust in Jesus' sacrifice.

2:16 'For assuredly he does not give help to angels, but he gives help to the seed of Abraham.'

Angels are by nature endowed with God's power, unlike men and women who start their relationship with God as helpless babes, unable to bring any good of themselves to the Father's service, but rather being fully dependent on him for everything. Those God 'helps' ('*epilambanomai*' - 'to take possession of' or 'lay hold of') are those who put their faith and trust in him, in the same way that Abraham did, and so are (by their faith) descendants ('*sperma*' - 'seed', 'offspring', or 'tribe of descendants') of Abraham. The KJV renders this verse differently - 'For verily he took not on *him the nature of* angels; but he took on *him* the seed of Abraham' - the italicised words are however additions to the Greek text. Of the other 19 uses of '*epilambanomai*' in the New Testament, all mean to 'take hold of something or someone', normally for a positive purpose. None of them use the word to mean taking on a different nature, therefore it is difficult to reconcile such a use in Hebrews 2:16. In Christ, God has 'taken hold of' us to help us. In all of the hundreds of references to angels in Scripture there are none where God is spoken of as 'helping' them or of taking hold on them to help them. Angels are powerful spirit-beings who chose to either use their power to serve God or to rebelliously oppose him.

2:17-18 'Therefore, he had to be made like his brethren in all things, so that he might become a merciful and faithful high priest in things pertaining to God, to make propitiation for the sins of the people. For since he himself was tempted in that which he has suffered, he is able to come to the aid of those who are tempted.'

Jesus is our model for life, our example of how to live as a family member in a relationship of trust with a heavenly father. He could be such a model because he was living as a fully human person, with fully human flesh and blood. Having overcome the Father's tests and the devil's temptations, he was ready to perform his priestly sacrifice as a perfect and mature son, one unstained by sin and so wholly acceptable to a holy God. 'Propitiation' here is '***hilaskomai***', meaning a 'merciful expiation and reconciliation', from '***hileôs***' [9] meaning 'mercy'.

Jesus' experience of the power of temptation in his own human body means that he can fully empathise with the struggles of our human lives. He is also well placed to help us overcome them, having overcome them himself. Jesus had a choice regarding whether or not to submit to the suffering of the crucifixion. He chose the Father's will over his own natural wish to avoid pain. Matthew 26:39-44: 'And he went a little beyond them, and fell on his face and prayed, saying, "My Father, if it is possible, let this cup pass from me; yet not as I will, but as you will." And he came to the disciples and found them sleeping, and said to Peter, "So, you men could not keep watch with me for one hour? Keep watching and praying that you may not enter into temptation; the spirit is willing, but the flesh is weak." He went away again a second time and prayed, saying, "My Father, if this cannot pass away unless I drink it, your will be done." Again he came and found them sleeping, for their eyes were heavy. And he left them again, and went away and prayed a third time, saying the same thing once more.' In passing that test ('temptation') he is qualified to help all those who face similar (though lesser) tests of their own. He is the greatest tutor for life, because he himself overcame life's greatest challenges in choosing his Father's will above all else. He is truly the 'Firstborn of many brethren'. And as our heavenly 'older brother' he is well-placed to empathise with our weaknesses and assist us in overcoming them.

Chapter 3

Consider Jesus - the 'prophet like Moses', only much greater - and hold onto him

3:1 'Therefore, holy brethren, partakers of a heavenly calling, consider Jesus, the Apostle and High Priest of our confession.'

'Consider' ('***katanoeô***' - 'perceive and take note of') Jesus.' How could anyone who has grasped what Jesus has done for mankind possibly not want to 'consider' him? Gaze upon him in wonder, love and praise. Reflect on him in all his glory. Admire and esteem him above all else for the love and mercy that he has shown us, the most undeserving of recipients.

The word 'Apostle' means 'one sent' on a mission, and is used by the Apostle John of Jesus - John 17:3: 'This is eternal life, that they may know you, the only true God, and Jesus Christ whom you *have sent*' ('***apostellô***'). Jesus' mission was a rescue-mission; he was sent behind enemy lines amongst hostile sinners to set us free from the one (the devil) who was imprisoning us in a world of sin. Jesus is also our High Priest, who offered his own blood in no less a place than the Holy of Holies in heaven itself. By comparison the one in the earthly temple was but a pale shadow, despite all the worldly glory that Herod's priest-builders (trained as 'tektons' almost certainly by Jesus' adoptive father Joseph, [10] that devout Judean tekton - Matthew 1:19 and 13:55) could bestow upon it. Our 'confession' is the faith that we 'profess' - '***homologeô***', meaning to 'speak out the same thing in agreement'. [11]

Our part as believers is to align ourselves in agreement with the word that God speaks to us, be it generally in regards to our relationship with him or particularly in regard to his will for us as individuals. Faith hears the particular word God speaks, and responds in active trust - 'Faith comes from hearing, and hearing by the word of Christ' (Romans 10:17). It is our agreement with and confession of that word that God speaks to us that catalyses the outworking of it in our lives. Jesus taught that 'If two of you agree on earth about anything that they may ask, it shall be done for them by my Father who is in heaven' (Matthew 18:19). As we enter into agreement with the word that God speaks to us, our trusting in it results in us 'saying the same thing' as God. This is '***homologeô***' - the 'confession' of faith over which the High Priesthood of Jesus presides for our good.

3:2-3 'He was faithful to him who appointed him, as Moses also was in all his house. For he has been counted worthy of more glory than Moses, by just so much as the builder of the house has more honour than the house.'

The writer quotes from Numbers 12:6-7, when the Lord spoke a word of rebuke to Aaron and Miriam following their criticism of Moses for his marriage to a Cushite woman. 'If there is a prophet among you, I, the Lord, shall make myself known to him in a vision, I shall speak with him in a dream. Not so with my servant Moses, he is faithful in all my household.' The Hebrew word for 'household' ('***bayith***') also means 'house', and the writer takes this opportunity to make a further comparison to the Lord Jesus Christ and a connection he had with the Lord's 'house' - the temple in Jerusalem.

Jesus was 100% faithful ('trusting himself to') to his Father's mission for him. He was indeed the promised 'prophet like Moses' (Deuteronomy 18:15). Having survived Pharaoh's murderous edict, Moses was raised as a highly educated person in the wisdom of the Egyptians, in the palace of Pharaoh, with his true identity and mission as an Israelite kept hidden from those around him. When it was eventually revealed, he was rejected by his own people. In just the same way, having survived Herod's murderous edict, Jesus' brilliance before the Doctors of the Law (Luke 2) would have inevitably led (in accordance with the Oral Jewish Law) to his rabbinic training in the education (Torah) of his people, in the splendid 'palace' that was the Temple of Herod. Yet Jesus' true identity as God's son was hidden, just as Moses' true Hebrew parentage was hidden.

When Jesus' true identity (equality with Yahweh) and mission (the forgiveness of sins) was revealed, he too was rejected by the leaders of his own people on grounds of blasphemy. Both Moses and Jesus returned from exile to complete their respective missions; Moses from Midian and Jesus from Hades (the place of the dead). Moses' father was not responsible for building the palace of Pharaoh, neither was Moses' mission (redemptive though it was) comparable with that of the Lord Jesus Christ.

How does 'the builder having more honour than the house' show that Jesus is greater than Moses? Because Jesus' adoptive father Joseph had trained the priests to do the work of '*tektons*' necessary in the construction of the Temple within the Court of the Priests (where none other than priests could go), Jesus could legally in that society accurately refer to the Temple as his 'Father's house'. This is why the Pharisees are unable to respond with the outrage due to such a provocative, and on the face of it, blasphemous remark as 'One greater than the Temple is here' (Matthew 12:6). They knew who Jesus' earthly father Joseph was and the role he had played in the construction of the Temple. The Jewish proverb quoted here in verse 3 ('The builder has more honour than the house') perfectly applied to Jesus as Joseph's eldest son and there was nothing that the Pharisees (Jewish religious lawyers) could say against it.

3:4-6 'For every house is built by someone, but the builder of all things is God. Now Moses was faithful in all his

house as a servant, for a testimony of those things which were to be spoken later; but Christ was faithful as a Son over his house, whose house we are, if we hold fast our confidence and the boast of our hope firm until the end.'

The Jews held that God was the one ultimately responsible for the (re)building of their Temple; indeed God's purposes were ultimately behind all things made. Jesus' earthly father's likely involvement in the construction puts him firmly in the plans and purposes of God. At this point in Jewish history the Temple had not yet met its demise at the hands of the Romans, as Jesus had foretold (Matthew 24). The writer does not refer to this destruction in any way, in fact its sacrifices are referred to as still being performed (Hebrews 10:11). Such a momentous happening as the destruction of the Holy Place could not fail to have been reflected in any Jew's writing at that time.

Once again the writer compares Moses (that greatest of Jewish lawgivers) unfavourably with the Lord Jesus Christ. Moses had overseen the construction of the Tabernacle; Jesus' earthly father had overseen the construction of the Temple (far more splendid than the Tent of Meeting). Jesus was a son rather than simply a servant like Moses. A servant has no choice other than to serve or be disciplined. A son who freely chooses to serve in a lowly way is truly a great-hearted son. Because in Christ we are in-dwelt by the person of the Holy Spirit, we are ourselves little temples of God. This is true individually (1 Corinthians 6:19: 'Do you not know that your body is a temple of the Holy Spirit who is in you, whom you have from God, and that you are not your own?'). It is also true collectively (1 Peter 2:5: 'You also, as living stones, are being built up as a spiritual house for a holy priesthood, to offer up spiritual sacrifices acceptable to God through Jesus Christ'). Jesus' work as a '***tekton***' continues in his church to this day, around himself as the cornerstone, which gives shape and solidity to the rest of the building. As Paul wrote to the Ephesians, 'Christ Jesus himself being the cornerstone, in whom the whole building, being fitted together, is growing into a holy temple in the Lord, in whom you also are being built together into a dwelling of God in the Spirit' (Ephesians 2:20-22). Peter also used this illustration of Jesus' temple building. 'Coming to him as to a living stone which has been rejected by men, but is choice and precious in the sight of God, you also, as living stones, are being built up as a spiritual house for a holy priesthood, to offer up spiritual sacrifices acceptable to God through Jesus Christ (1 Peter 2:4-5). Jesus is still about his Father's business of building his church.

There is a need to show (to ourselves as much as anyone else) that we, like both Moses and Jesus, are faithful to the 'confidence' we have in him. This is '***parrêsia***', meaning 'a boldness in freedom of speech' - no mealy-mouthedness here! - and 'hope' ('***elpis***' - a 'confident expectation') that we have taken hold of, or perhaps rather that has taken hold of us.

3:7-11 'Therefore, just as the Holy Spirit says, "Today, if you hear his voice, do not harden your hearts as when they provoked me, as in the day of trial in the wilderness, where your fathers tried me by testing me, and saw my works for forty years. Therefore I was angry with this generation, and said, "They always go astray in their heart, and they did not know my ways, as I swore in my wrath, 'They shall not enter my rest.'"'

Starting a journey is not the same as finishing it. The people of Israel, journeying through the wilderness, managed to prolong their journey-time as a result of their unbelief such that only Joshua and Caleb survived to see the finishing-line. God is quite willing to lead us in circular patterns while we learn a necessary lesson. The Greek perfect tense of 'saved' in Ephesians 2:5 ('By grace you have been saved'), means that it is a process with a start (a new birth), a middle (sanctification and Christ-likeness) and an end (arrival in heaven complete with a new body). Only then is the process of 'being saved' completed. If we hold on to God (who is holding onto us while also respecting our freewill) then we can be assured of stage three which by definition has yet to happen for any of us on earth. We are the only people who can interfere with our own salvation, and it is extremely rare that anyone would want to! But the prospect of becoming 'hardened' ('***sklêrunô***', from which is derived the term 'sclerosis', used in regard to hardening of the body's arteries) in our hearts is one that everyone faces, because sin is still at large and sin's power is one that is able to harden even the hearts of redeemed men and women. As Philippians 2:12 says, we should 'work out our own salvation with fear and trembling'.

The writer then quotes from Psalm 95:8-11 (itself describing the consequences of the events of Exodus 17:1-7) [v] : 'Do not harden your hearts, as at Meribah, as in the day of Massah in the wilderness, "When your fathers tested me, they tried me, though they had seen my work. For forty years I loathed that generation, and said they are

---

[v] Exodus 17:1-7 'Then all the congregation of the sons of Israel journeyed by stages from the wilderness of Sin, according to the command of the Lord, and camped at Rephidim, and there was no water for the people to drink. Therefore the people quarrelled with Moses and said, "Give us water that we may drink." And Moses said to them, "Why do you quarrel with me? Why do you test the Lord?" But the people thirsted there for water; and they grumbled against Moses and said, "Why now have you brought us up from Egypt, to kill us and our children and our livestock with thirst?" So Moses cried out to the Lord saying, "What shall I do to this people? A little more and they will stone me." Then the Lord said to Moses, "Pass before the people and take with you some of the elders of Israel, and take in your hand your staff with which you struck the Nile, and go. Behold, I will stand before you there on the rock at Horeb; and you shall strike the rock, and water will come out of it, that the people may drink." And Moses did so in the sight of the elders of Israel. He named the place Massah and Meribah because of the quarrel of the sons of Israel, and because they tested the Lord, saying, "Is the Lord among us, or not?"'

a people who err in their heart, and they do not know my ways. Therefore I swore in my anger, "Truly they shall not enter into my rest."' The nation of Israel serves as a chilling illustration of such a hardening of the spiritual cardiac arteries. Miraculously delivered from slavery in Egypt, they find the process of hardening beginning over matters as trite as cucumbers (Numbers 11:5). Such acts of sinful rebellion, as shortly followed from people such as even Miriam and Aaron (Numbers 12:2), are provocative to a holy God. Thus precipitated, God's consequential anger (in sending a plague over the people as they gorged themselves on quail and afflicting Miriam temporarily with leprosy) were expressions of God's fatherly discipline. The children of Israel went into circular motion on a long and sun-baked desert hike that lasted until the culprits had all died out. Only then did God allow those who had remained faithful (such as Joshua and Caleb) to enter the Promised Land. The 'rest' there (after overcoming the resident opposition) is symbolic of the eternal rest in heaven that awaits us all at life's journey's end. God's discipline will deny us rest until we repent and resume normal service.

'Rest' now becomes a central theme. When God finished his work of creation, he rested. Genesis 2:1-3 records: 'Thus the heavens and the earth were completed, and all their hosts. By the seventh day God completed his work which he had done, and he rested on the seventh day from all his work which he had done. Then God blessed the seventh day and sanctified it, because in it he rested from all his work which God had created and made.' What is missing from the creation narrative, in contrast to the first 6 days, is the usual reference to the evening closing the seventh day. This signifies a sense that God's rest is not supposed to be viewed as something that has ceased; rather it lives on. All that God will do has from his perspective (outside of time) already happened. We are offered the opportunity to join with him in his rest, for example, resting from sin and from striving to please him in our own efforts rather than by relying on him and joining in with what he is doing by his Spirit.

3:12-13 'Take care, brethren, that there not be in any one of you an evil, unbelieving heart that falls away from the living God. But encourage one another day after day, as long as it is still called 'Today', so that none of you will be hardened by the deceitfulness of sin.'

The warning of the people of Israel's mistakes and sin should serve as instruction to us to avoid making the same mistakes. We are called to examine our own hearts (where Christ dwells by faith - Ephesians 3:17) to check that they are aligned with the compass of his Spirit. Mutual encouragement ('***parakaleô***' - the ministry of the Holy Spirit in 'coming alongside' to help) is important in this regard, while time remains in which to do so ('today'). Once again, sin's inherent power to deceive and harden is brought to our attention. There is no deception as widespread as self-deception, and human nature is a master of that art.

3:14-15 'For we have become partakers of Christ if we hold fast the beginning of our assurance firm until the end, while it is said, "Today if you hear his voice do not harden your hearts as when they provoked me."

The evidence of true 'partaking' ('partnering in') conversion and new birth is faithfulness and faith, which is what enables us to hold fast to the head - Christ (Colossians 2:19). The glue of that relationship cannot come unstuck, whatever life's corrosive trials may throw at it. Once again Psalm 95 is quoted; when God's voice is heard, we have a choice. We can either receive his word in faith and trust (this does not discount testing it as part of any guidance received from any source), or we can reject it and in doing so harden our own hearts making ourselves increasingly deaf to the voice of our heavenly shepherd. The Pharisees were able to 'provoke' Jesus' spirit by their unbelieving questions (Mark 8:11, Luke 11:53), and our unbelieving responses to God can inadvertently have the same effect. This is something that the writer to the Hebrews is keen that both we and they avoid.

3:16-17 'For who provoked him when they had heard? Indeed, did not all those who came out of Egypt led by Moses? And with whom was he angry for forty years? Was it not with those who sinned, whose bodies fell in the wilderness?'

The people of Israel's eagerness to join in their frequent rebellions (e.g. the golden calf of Exodus 32) was evidence of the fact that their hearts had remained fundamentally unchanged despite witnessing God's interventional deliverance at the parting of the Red Sea. As believers in Jesus we have a huge advantage over them; we are in-dwelt of the Holy Spirit and so have a powerful person within us who can do the work of change, with our cooperation. With his help there is no need to fear that the same outcome that befell the rebellious Israelites will befall us. They indeed sustained forty years of discipline until those responsible had all died, with only Joshua and Caleb proving faithful and so able to enter the Promised Land. God's loving fatherly care committed him to discipline his children and still does so.

3:18-19 'And to whom did he swear that they would not enter his rest, but to those who were disobedient? So we see that they were not able to enter because of unbelief.'

Disobedience, as with any truly caring parent, will lead to lovingly imparted discipline. God cares about our future characters and heavenly reward too much for us to be left to wallow in our sin. He will lead us, if we trustingly place our hand in his, into the place of ultimate 'rest' from sin, heaven itself. Before that, he invites us to a stress-free faith/trust-inspired walk with him which is the walk that Jesus modelled for us to imitate - one in step with his Father's Spirit. Rest comes from the sort of 'trusting' and the 'leaning' on God that Proverbs 3:5 commands, [vi] free of the outworking of unbelief ('unfaithfulness'). Fear/anxiety keep us from that rest; faith/trust bring us into it.

[vi] Proverbs 3:5-6: 'Trust in the Lord with all your heart, and do not lean on your own understanding. In all your ways acknowledge him, and he will make your paths straight.'

Chapter 4

God's rest and our rest - the disposition of faith

4:1-2 'Therefore let us fear if, while a promise remains of entering his rest, any one of you may seem to have come short of it. For indeed we have had good news preached to us, just as they also; but the word they heard did not profit them, because it was not united by faith in those who heard.'

The state of 'rest' that faith brings is for this life as well as for the next. There is a godly fear and awe of God that leads us into that place of faith. The Greek for 'fear' here is '*phobeô*', meaning a healthy sense of respect that helps prompt us towards the disposition of obedience. 'The fear of the Lord is the beginning of wisdom; all who follow his precepts have good understanding' (Psalm 111:10, NIV).

Sin causes us to fall short of God's glory, in the sense of the likeness of God in us and our participation in and enjoyment of all that God has prepared for us. ('All have sinned and fall short of the glory of God' - Romans 3:23.) Lack of trust also causes us to fall short of the place of 'rest' in our faith-inspired walk with God. The 'good news' of God's kingdom rule has been proclaimed and a response made, but the full good of that will only be experienced by us in this life if it is met by an attitude of faith and trust that goes further into our on-going daily experience. 'United' here is '*sugkerannumi*', meaning to 'co-mingle' from '*kerannumi*', meaning to mix two things together so that 'the two become one'. [12] Saving faith is the gift of God (Ephesians 2:8), and it is generated by hearing the word he speaks in an attitude of trust and a willingness to obey it - 'faith comes by hearing, and hearing by the word of God' (Romans 10:17, KJV). It was faith (trust in action) that propelled Peter out of the boat on storm-tossed Lake Galilee (Matthew 14:29). Our own attitude of willing receptivity to the word of God, mixing the hearing of God's word with trust and an obedient response is vital in fostering the response of faith that God enables within us.

4:3 'For we who have believed enter that rest, just as he has said, "As I swore in my wrath, they shall not enter my rest", although his works were finished from the foundation of the world.'

Re-visiting Psalm 95, God's perspective as a Being who dwells in heaven, outside of our realm of created matter and time, is again referred to in regard to his finished works. All of God's works, from his perspective, have already been completed. The six days of work that Genesis chapter 1 records were not simply devoted to the material creation, God had also forethought of all that he would accomplish through his people. As Paul wrote to the Ephesians (2:10), 'For we are his workmanship, created in Christ Jesus for good works, which God prepared beforehand so that we would walk in them.' These 'good works' of God (that he has prepared for us to do in his name) have also been known by him 'from the foundation of the world.' Our part is to 'walk in them.' God invites us to enter into rest from struggling to work for him in our own strength and instead to allow him to work through us as we lean on him in the attitude of trust and dependency that Proverbs 3:5 commands: 'Trust in the Lord with all your heart and do not lean on your own understanding.'

God is still at work within our experience of time and space but, unlike us, is able to see the end and the beginning simultaneously. From his perspective outside of time, everything that will ever happen in our world has already happened. We can choose to be part of his works through the exercise of faith and trust. This attitude of faith and trust is not one that comes naturally. If we choose not to trust, perhaps out of hardness of heart or laziness, God has already seen that and has already taken that into account in determining and carrying out his will. We are the ones that lose out by allowing our hearts to be hardened. While we may miss out in terms of heavenly and eternal reward, God's eternal purposes, based on his perfect will, are still fulfilled.

4:4-6 'For he has said somewhere concerning the seventh day: 'And God rested on the seventh day from all his works', and again in this passage, 'They shall not enter my rest.' Therefore, since it remains for some to enter it, and those who formerly had good news preached to them failed to enter because of disobedience.'

Once again, 'somewhere' means 'Where?'; and is being asked in a rhetorical manner in the sense of acknowledging that his audience is familiar with the text concerned. The verse in question was very well known to all Jews, being the creation narrative of Genesis 2:2. Here God finishes his work of creation and sets apart the Sabbath day of rest for his people to follow. All are supposed to follow his example by participating in the 'work' of faith (in receiving his gracious gift of new heavenly birth), with the 'rest' of faith being a life lived out through a disposition of trust in his leadership and guidance. Because we are conditioned by society to trust in ourselves rather than in God, we often rely on our own abilities rather than in the God who gave us those abilities in the first place. This 'disobedience' to God's declared intention that we 'trust in the Lord with all our hearts and lean not on our own understanding' (Proverbs 3:5) means that we can miss out on God's provision by attempting to substitute for it a provision of our own making. We then fail to enter into all the good that God has stored up for us.

4:7-9 'He again fixes a certain day, 'Today'; saying through David after so long a time just as has been said before,

"Today, if you hear his voice, do not harden your hearts." For if Joshua had given them rest, he would not have spoken of another day after that. So there remains a Sabbath rest for the people of God.'

Again, the writer alludes to Psalm 95 and the heart condition that prevents us from receiving God's word with an active trust and so coming into the place of rest that faith makes possible. Joshua had not been able to bring God's people under the Old Covenant into a place of faith and rest, but his namesake Y'shua would by means of his example, his saving sacrifice at Calvary and his life-giving Spirit. The fact that God's Spirit has now been poured out on 'all flesh' (Joel 2:28), means that God is now working in an even clearer way and pointing to his Son's sacrifice at Calvary. This is a much more powerful voice than David's, God-inspired though his was. God is speaking to all humanity by his Spirit. 'He sends forth his command to the earth; his word runs very swiftly' (Psalm 147:15). If we hear, listen, trust and obey we will experience the blessings of God showing up in our lives in an on-going way that illustrates the purpose of the Sabbath - rest and relationship with God. Serving God is not supposed to be like walking through treacle. It is supposed to be the relatively easy process of walking into the good works that God has already prepared for us to participate in, with him, just as any Jewish father would allow his sons (and all God's children are 'sons') to participate with him in learning their father's trade.

4:10-11 'For the one who has entered his rest has himself also rested from his works, as God did from his. Therefore let us be diligent to enter that rest, so that no one will fall through following the same example of disobedience.'

The 'rest' of faith means that we cease trying to do things (our own 'works') for God in our own strength and instead start to flow with what God is already doing; or rather has already done and now waits for us to 'walk into' (good works prepared in advance). [vii] This means joining in with him in an attitude of relaxed trust that depends on him rather than ourselves ('Unless the Lord builds the house, they labour in vain who build it' - Psalm 127:1). Because life in our fallen world conditions us to be self-dependent rather than God-dependent, it takes diligence on our part to remain in a place of leaning on him rather than on our own strengths and abilities, good and God-given though they are.

'Diligence' here is '***spoudazô***', meaning 'to earnestly hasten to accomplish something', [13] in this case the disposition of faith needed to lean upon God rather than on ourselves and on our own abilities. The RSV's choice of 'strive' to translate '***spoudazô***' can imply the opposite to the 'rest' that God intends, even though it is to be sought with diligent haste and endeavour. Because all of humanity tends towards relying on its own efforts, there is a sense in which a diligent effort has to be made to realise the disposition of faith that is fundamentally counter-intuitive to human nature. The disobedience of self-reliance rather than God-reliance is an example set by the people of Israel that we would do well not to follow.

4:12 'For the word of God is living and active and sharper than any two-edged sword, and piercing as far as the division of soul and spirit, of both joints and marrow, and able to judge the thoughts and intentions of the heart.'

This verse can be read in two ways, firstly as applying to the Scripture, but also to applying to the '*logos*' made flesh [viii] - the Lord Jesus himself. The Book of Revelation (1:16) contains this

---

[vii] Ephesians 2:10: 'We are his workmanship, created in Christ Jesus for good works, which God prepared beforehand so that we would walk in them.'

[viii] John 1:14 'The Word became flesh, and dwelt among us.'

description of the risen Christ: 'In his right hand he held seven stars, and out of his mouth came a sharp two-edged sword; and his face was like the sun shining in its strength.'

Faith is generated as a response in our hearts to the word God speaks to us. As has been said, when Jesus spoke one word ('Come') in response to Peter's appeal to him in a storm on Lake Galilee, it was sufficient to ignite the gift of faith in Peter's heart through his pre-disposition to trust. The subsequent explosion of power propelled Peter against all natural instinct and reason to climb out of the boat and onto the wind-driven waves. God's word always has power to create and ignite faith in the hearts and lives of the hearers. Its scalpel-like sharpness can divide things that appear on the surface to be one and the same.

'Soul' here is ***psuchê***', meaning 'breath' in the sense of our human life. 'Spirit' is ***pneuma***', also meaning 'breath', but in the sense of breath from God, commonly denoting his Spirit, or simply 'Breath from God', as in Revelation 11:11. 'The breath of life from God came into them, and they stood on their feet'. Breath is synonymous in Scripture with life; when a person died they stopped breathing. God's breath became our breath, hence the two thoughts are closely linked, but not so closely that God's word cannot divide them. In the same way skeletal joints are closely attached to the marrow of the bones that they connect. There is similarly a very small step between 'thought' ('consideration' or 'pondering') and 'intentions' that carry the sense of a 'purpose' or 'design'. [14] A small step, but not so small that the Lord Jesus and the word he speaks cannot divide it.

4:13 'And there is no creature hidden from his sight, but all things are open and laid bare to the eyes of him with whom we have to do.'

The writers' use of the possessive pronoun supports the idea that the reference to 'the word of God' in verse 12 is actually about the person of Christ. God is all seeing. He can see what we sometimes cannot - where the weight of our dependency is situated - on him and his word, or upon ourselves and our own plans, strength and abilities. He will not bless that which is of ourselves alone, because 'that which is not of faith is sin' (Romans 14:23).

4:14-16 'Therefore, since we have a great high priest who has passed through the heavens, Jesus the Son of God, let us hold fast our confession. For we do not have a high priest who cannot sympathize with our weaknesses, but one who has been tempted in all things as we are, yet without sin. Therefore let us draw near with confidence to the throne of grace, so that we may receive mercy and find grace to help in time of need.'

Jesus is now very clearly revealed as the one who is himself the 'Word made flesh' (John 1:14). Fortunately for us he, our advocate in heaven, knows exactly what it is like to be human and so be prone to making the mistakes that humans can make, whilst being himself without any sin. Once a year the High Priest would pass through the Holy Place and enter the Holy of Holies, but not without first having purified himself of his own sin. Our much greater High Priest has passed through heaven itself to present the spotless sacrifice of his own life before his Father. Jesus, the one person who might have been entitled to self-reliance in his own nature in the Godhead, modelled dependency on his heavenly Father, saying that 'The Father loves the Son, and shows him all things that he himself is doing' (John 5:20). And again, 'I can of mine own self do nothing; as I hear, I judge, and my judgment is just; because I seek not mine own will, but the will of the Father which hath sent me' (John 5:30, KJV). Having been tempted by the Devil in the wilderness (Luke chapter 4) to rely upon himself instead, he can sympathize with us when we are similarly inclined to self-dependency. We are invited to depend on the Father in the same way that Jesus did.

'Confession' is, once again, '***homologeô***' - to 'speak out the same thing in agreement'. Our response to God's word to us may well be tested, just as Peter was distracted from the faith engendering word that Christ had spoken to him ('Come!') by the wind and waves of Lake Galilee.

'Hold fast' our faith/confession is '***krateô***', meaning to 'powerfully take hold of something in order to master it'. [15] The more powerfully we take hold of God's word to us in faith and trust, the more effective we will be as Christians. Jesus is able to fully understand and empathise with our human weakness based on his own personal experience in becoming human and experiencing the same sorts of tests and temptations that we do. There is indeed a throne of grace, favour and delight that he sits upon, and from which he rules on our behalf and for our renewal. 'He that sat upon the throne said, "Behold, I make all things new"' (Revelation 21:5, KJV).

Rather than stop at simply forgiving our sins, God is ever willing to come to our assistance with mercy and help, whenever and whatever our need. We are not given what we do deserve but rather we are given what we do not deserve. This act of grace means that we may adopt a disposition of confidence (not at all the same thing as presumption), reflecting the faith and trust that knows that God is for us, not against us. And 'If God is for us, who is against us?' (Romans 8:31). God is always 'for' us and not 'against' us, just as any loving father is favourably disposed towards his own children. We can therefore stand in faith, confident in the fact that he is for us, and not allow ourselves to be robbed of the sense of self-worth that this invokes in us.

Chapter 5

Jesus - our great High Priest

5:1-4 'For every high priest taken from among men is appointed on behalf of men in things pertaining to God, in order to offer both gifts and sacrifices for sins; he can deal gently with the ignorant and misguided, since he himself also is beset with weakness; and because of it he is obligated to offer sacrifices for sins, as for the people, so also for himself. And no one takes the honour to himself, but receives it when he is called by God, even as Aaron was.'

The writer returns to reflecting on how much greater than any earthly human high priest Jesus is. Despite his exalted position of co-equality within the triune Godhead Jesus was prepared to obey his Father and submit to the indignities and restrictions of the incarnation, lowering himself into a human embryo to be born and therefore able, like the high priest, to personally comprehend the difficulties that men and women experience in seeking to please a holy God. Just as no person could take such a priestly office upon themselves (the priests had to be born into the right family and then chosen by the Sanhedrin, the ruling Jewish council), so Jesus was called to the role of an incarnate mediator by his heavenly Father, an appointment made by the whole Godhead in the courts of heaven.

5:5-6 'So also Christ did not glorify himself so as to become a high priest, but he who said to him, "You are my Son; today I have begotten you", just as he says also in another passage, "You are a priest forever, according to the order of Melchizedek."'

Jesus' eternal sonship, integral to the nature and person of God, is unique to him alone. His role includes kingship, after the nature of his heavenly Father, and priesthood in his work of mediating between God and mankind through his own sacrifice. In 'begetting' Jesus, rather than creating him (Psalm 2:7), the Father called him to tangibly express his divine sonship with the particular purpose of providing a perfect yet tangibly human example for us to follow. Jesus' sonship also embodied the role of priest (after the order of Melchizedek, Psalm 110:4) with a much greater nature than established under Aaron. For there had been an earlier priesthood in the history of the people of God. This was Melchizedek (Genesis 14:18-20: 'Priest of God most high'), who had an authority that their founding patriarch Abraham (at that time called Abram) had recognised and offered a tithe to. It is to this more ancient and greater order of priesthood (see chapter 7) that Jesus belongs.

5:7-9 'In the days of his flesh, he offered up both prayers and supplications with loud crying and tears to the One able to save him from death, and he was heard because of his piety. Although he was a Son, he learned obedience from the things which he suffered. And having been made perfect, he became to all those who obey him the source of eternal salvation.'

Jesus' intercessions might be thought of as being for himself, so that he might be 'saved from death'. It is certainly true that the pain of the crucifixion was not something that any sane person would want, and Christ did need to align himself with his Father's will in that regard ('Father, if you are willing, remove this cup from me; yet not my will, but yours be done' - Luke 22:42). However, Jesus had perfect trust in his Father's ability to fulfil Psalm 116 and so save him from the power of death. 'The cords of death entangled me, the anguish of the grave came upon me; I was overcome by trouble and sorrow. Then I called on the name of the Lord, "Oh Lord save me!" The Lord is gracious and righteous; our God is full of compassion. The Lord protects the simple hearted; when I was in great need, he saved me. Be at rest once more, O my soul, for the Lord has been good to you. For you, O Lord, have delivered my soul from death, my eyes from tears, my feet from stumbling' (Psalm 116:3-8, NIV).

The idea that Jesus' prayers were designed to save him from a death that he knew by his own nature and being could not possibly separate him from his Father, contradicts his own willingness to submit to the Father's plan. The plan to save mankind was known to Jesus from before the foundation of the world, and in Gethsemane Jesus was not having second thoughts about his participation in it. Rather he was steeling himself to win the mental battle necessary to go through the trials and suffering that awaited him in a disposition of trust, the same trust that had marked every step he had taken to that point of his life on earth.

The 'prayers and supplications' mentioned here are indeed offered to the 'One able to save him from death', but not in the sense of requesting that he be spared the death of the cross. Jesus knew that there was no other way to save mankind, and he had an eternity earlier made up his mind to do just that. Jesus always prayed to the 'One able to save him from death'. Who else was there to pray to? His prayer was not to be spared his Father's will but to be strengthened to go through it, in complete trust in his Father's ability to stay with him in it and to defeat the power of death over humanity by his resurrection. Truly God (the Father) was in Christ reconciling the world to himself, at Calvary. And strengthening was just what he received; Luke tells us that 'An angel from heaven appeared to him, strengthening him' (Luke 22:43).

Jesus' obedience to his Father's call to suffer in our place and in so doing bear the penalty and punishment for sin due to us is what contributed to this 'perfection' ('***teleioô***' - 'to bring to completion') or maturity as a son, the ultimate final development in what he was modelling for us to follow him into. The salvation process of recycling perishing and fallen men and women into saints of God has not ceased since that time. Jesus' sacrifice was the source and point of access for all the good that God has in store for us to receive.

5:10-11 'Being designated by God as a high priest according to the order of Melchizedek. Concerning him we have much to say, and it is hard to explain, since you have become dull of hearing.'

'Designated' is '***prosagoreuô***', meaning to 'publically call by name in the assembly'. Addressed as high priest by God the Father, some have unfortunately become too deaf to hear the title. Spiritual deafness was something that badly afflicted the Judean Jews at the time of Jesus. Matthew records (13:15, NIV): 'For this people's heart has become calloused; they hardly hear with their ears, and they have closed their eyes.' This condition, also prevalent at the time of Isaiah (Isaiah 6:10), can be caused by sin or by an over-feeding on truth without utilising the grace and energy received in God's service - overfed and obese people do not make natural runners for the race of life.

The writer now turns his attention once more to the greater nature of Jesus' high priesthood compared to that of Aaron. Jesus' birth into the tribe of Judah, along with the whole concept of the incarnation, was a source of stumbling for those Jews who expected a priestly role from the promised Messiah, despite the prophecies that Messiah would be from the lineage of David. Melchizedek was a somewhat shadowy figure in Jewish history, a non-Jew who appeared briefly in the life of their forefather Abraham and then disappeared again just as quickly. Consequently the writer feels that his appearance will be hard to explain, particularly given the possibly typical 'know-it-all' attitude of his Jewish audience.

5:12-14 'For though by this time you ought to be teachers, you have need again for someone to teach you the elementary principles of the oracles of God, and you have come to need milk and not solid food. For everyone who partakes only of milk is not accustomed to the word of righteousness, for he is an infant. But solid food is for the mature, who because of practice have their senses trained to discern good and evil.'

The spiritually well-fed Jewish audience ought to have been using their knowledge by passing it on to those less well-informed. There is often reluctance on the part of some in the church today to get their hands dirty with the kingdom business of evangelism (many would prefer to pay someone else to do this on their behalf). This is symptomatic of the all-too-human attitude of wanting to receive but then being reluctant to be involved with the work of passing it on. So they quickly became full and obese, contributing to the spiritual hardening of the arteries that Jesus has warned of (Matthew 13:15). [ix] They had relapsed into a baby-state, needing to begin again with the basics, the milk of God's word, rather than the solid food associated with more grown-up members of the family. Force-feeding solid food on babies will only cause the babies to choke.

Many of the priests and leaders of Jesus' day had dissociated themselves from ordinary society, adopting an attitude of contempt to those whose life circumstances did not allow them to learn the Oral Torah well enough to be said to be keeping it. They regarded such (albeit religious) Jews as sinners to be avoided on grounds of religious purity, as may be seen from the disparaging remark made

---

[ix] Matthew 13:15 'For this people's heart is waxed gross, and their ears are dull of hearing, and their eyes they have closed; lest at any time they should see with their eyes, and hear with their ears, and should understand with their heart, and should be converted, and I should heal them.'

about the crowd of Jewish worshippers at the Feast of Tabernacles. 'This crowd which does not know the Law is accursed' (John 7:49).

The teaching of God's word has the primary intention of producing 'love from a pure heart and a good conscience and a sincere faith' (1 Timothy 1:5). Mature folk have had some 'practice' (Greek: '***hexis***' - 'a habit or power of body or mind acquired by custom, practice and use') [16] in discerning good and evil. They have doubtless made some mistakes and learned from them as well. That too can benefit babies; it is always less painful to learn from other's errors than from your own! Going your 'own way' is unwise if the way in question is littered with the casualties of those who have gone that way before you.

Chapter 6

Jesus' gift of hope - anchored in heaven

6:1-3 'Therefore leaving the elementary teaching about the Christ, let us press on to maturity, not laying again a foundation of repentance from dead works and of faith toward God, of instruction about washings and laying on of hands, and the resurrection of the dead and eternal judgment. And this we will do, if God permits.'

For the writer to the Hebrews, the basics of faith included such things as 'instructions about washings'. These are elements of the Mosaic Law that the early Jewish followers of Jesus were continuing to observe, presumably because they saw them as reflecting an underlying truth that they were keen to recognise. 'Washings' here is '*baptismos*' and it was these Jewish practices that provided the basis for Christian water baptism. Early Christian baptism followed the Jewish pattern of total immersion (where sufficient water was available), and the writer's audience would have been familiar with the '*mikvah*' baths used for ritual purification by self-immersion that existed outside the Temple for worshippers to use prior to entry, based upon the command to Moses concerning the Priests. 'When they enter the tent of meeting, they shall wash with water, so that they will not die' (Exodus 30:20). The Temple itself contained underground pools for the Priests use at the start of each day's service. [17] Once that had occurred they only had to wash their hands and feet to be regarded as legally clean. This is likely to be the background to Jesus' saying (John 13:10), 'He who has bathed needs only to wash his feet, but is completely clean.' The plurality of 'baptisms' points to its use extending beyond water baptism to the baptism in the Holy Spirit that Jesus spoke of in Acts 1:5 ('John baptized with water, but you will be baptized with the Holy Spirit not many days from now'). 'Baptism' carries with it the concept of a change in nature; Jesus' followers were changed from being scared disciples of an executed Jewish Torah teacher into indomitable men and women whose Spirit-empowered testimonies changed the world.

'Repentance from dead works' is also listed as a basic element of Christian initiation and teaching; 'dead' is '***nekros***' (as in 'necrotic' - dead and rotting). These works produce frustration rather than fulfilment and fruit, and reflect the 'old' ways that the new life in Christ is designed to supersede, but which the old nature ('the flesh') is reluctant to let go of. 'Laying on of hands' here probably represents both the process of appointing to ministry under the Jewish pattern of rabbinic ordination ('***semicha***'), and also the prayers and blessings that would accompany baptismal 'washings', rather than prayer (for example for healing) in general.

'The resurrection of the dead and eternal judgment' represents the 'last things' which human life is intended to be conducted in the light of. Heaven and hell are the only two end-points for humanity that Scripture presents; where we will end up is in our own hands. Once such truths have been inwardly digested then the writer encourages us to press on towards maturity. The Greek here is '***teleiotês***' - 'perfection', meaning to grow up in God and fulfil the potential that he has placed in each one of us from before the creation of the world, when we were foreknown in the mind of our Creator.

6:4-8 'For in the case of those who have once been enlightened and have tasted of the heavenly gift and have been made partakers of the Holy Spirit, and have tasted the good word of God and the powers of the age to come, and then have fallen away, it is impossible to renew them again to repentance, since they again crucify to themselves the Son of God and put him to open shame. For ground that drinks the rain which often falls on it and

brings forth vegetation useful to those for whose sake it is also tilled, receives a blessing from God; but if it yields thorns and thistles, it is worthless and close to being cursed, and it ends up being burned.'

Having encouraged his hearers to press on towards maturity, the writer turns his attention to those who had abandoned the fledgling church and returned to Judaism, which formally regarded Christ himself as an apostate from the faith and Law that he has been ordained to represent, and as one who had died apparently under God's curse (Deuteronomy 21:23). Having become 'partakers of the Holy Spirit' they had most certainly been 'born again'; there is no room for the idea that they might not have been numbered in the people of God's new covenant. How could they be brought to a place of repentance ('*metanoia*' - 'a change of mind')? Was it worth trying to? The answer is 'no'; humanly speaking there is nothing further to do. Fortunately that does not exclude the intervention of Almighty God. The passage does not state that it is not possible for God to intervene and bring them to forgiveness; hence this is a very different thing to the 'blasphemy against the Holy Spirit' that Jesus warned of (Matthew 12:31). What is impossible for men to achieve is all too possible for God (Mark 10:27).

Land that produced thorns was hard to pasture; the seeds of the thorn's weeds were too resistant. The common practice was to burn the soil, thereby destroying the seeds. The soil could then be re-fertilised and good seed planted. The 'scorched-earth' policy such as employed by retreating Soviet armies only served to make the land unproductive for a time; it would always eventually recover and become fruitful again, as God intended. 'Close to being cursed' is not quite the same as actually being cursed. Only when the names are read out in heaven itself will we know who responded to God's constant supply of grace and who did not. Jesus was put to 'open shame' outside the gate of Jerusalem, and is unfortunately also put to shame by Christians who do not lay hold of the fullness of life that he offers but persist in lack of faith by relying on themselves to do the works of God in their own strength. Fortunately their self-imposed disqualification does not need to permanently prevent them from participating in the sort of fruitful kingdom service that God intends. The believers' works will be tested as to whether they are born of God. 'If any man builds on the foundation with gold, silver, precious stones, wood, hay, straw, each man's work will become evident; for the day will show it, because it is to be revealed with fire, and the fire itself will test the quality of each man's work. If any man's work which he has built on it remains, he will receive a reward. If any man's work is burned up, he will suffer loss; but he himself will be saved, yet so as through fire' (1 Corinthians 3:12-15). The works that are born of God in active trust and faith are represented by 'gold, silver and precious stones.' They will last for eternity and bring glory to the God who prepared them to be walked into in the first place.

6:9-10 'But, beloved, we are convinced of better things concerning you, and things that accompany salvation, though we are speaking in this way. For God is not unjust so as to forget your work and the love which you have shown toward his name, in having ministered and in still ministering to the saints.'

Having got the warning about burned soil out of his system, the writer returns to the 'better things' that he knows the Father has in store for his children if they respond to his gentle leadership. Much good fruit has already been produced; evidence itself of the gift of love that his children have received from him. Salvation is accompanied by the fruit and the many gifts of the Spirit (Hebrews 2:4). Everything that God has wrought in and through the lives of his children has been written in his book awaiting the day of reward (2

Timothy 4:8), [x] when those whose names are written on the palms of his hands will receive the blessing prepared for them from before the foundation of the world. God, the righteous judge (2 Timothy 4:8), rewards as well as punishes and disciplines, but as a Father towards his blood-bought children he is much more inclined towards favour. The 'saints' ('***hagios***' - 'holy ones') are always worth ministering to (for example, the widows of Acts 6:1 and the Judean poor of 2 Corinthians 9:1). As we give to God in this way so God gives back to us, and in a much greater measure. (Luke 6:38: "Give, and it will be given to you. They will pour into your lap a good measure - pressed down, shaken together, and running over. For by your standard of measure it will be measured to you in return.") God's word has always reflected the concern he has for the poor and disadvantaged. 'One who is gracious to a poor man lends to the Lord, and he will repay him for his good deed' (Proverbs 19:17). This was evident in the early church, as Galatians 2:10 makes clear, 'They (*the apostles*) only asked us (*Paul, Barnabas and Titus*) to remember the poor - the very thing I also was eager to do.'

6:11-12 'And we desire that each one of you show the same diligence so as to realize the full assurance of hope until the end, so that you will not be sluggish, but imitators of those who through faith and patience inherit the promises.'

Once again, 'diligence' (the Greek is '***spoudē***' - 'earnestness') and perseverance are called forth out of the hearers, in order that they may attain the confidence of 'hope' ('***elpis***' - a 'confident expectation of good') that is the rightful inheritance of all of God's

---

[x] 2 Timothy 4:8 'There is laid up for me the crown of righteousness, which the Lord, the righteous Judge, will award to me on that day; and not only to me, but also to all who have loved his appearing.'

children. Being 'sluggish' ('slothful') and lazy simply reduces the degree of reward to be received from God, the righteous judge. God desires that we live in the reality of this diligence to the end - that we finish the race well. If we fall, what is important is that we get back up and keep on going. The apostles' example and those of the saints referred to in chapter 11 are good ways of copying a faith-based lifestyle. Their 'faith' and 'patience' are reasons for their spiritual success and fruitfulness; they have not 'left their first love', as Jesus reproached the church at Ephesus for doing (Revelation 2:4).

6:13-15 'For when God made the promise to Abraham, since he could swear by no one greater, he swore by himself, saying, "I will surely bless you, and multiply you." And so, having patiently waited, he obtained the promise.'

Abraham had believed God's promise to him (Genesis 22:17) concerning his descendants, and that had been 'counted to him as righteousness' (Romans 4:3); this had made him 'the friend of God' (James 2:23). [xi] But Abraham had still to wait for the fulfilment of the promise. Unfortunately he lacked the 'patience' advocated by the writer to the Hebrews and decided to take matters (and more particularly his wife's maid, Hagar - Genesis 16:4), [xii] into his own hands. At a crucial moment of testing, Abraham failed the test. The world is still paying the price for this sin and lack of trust in the One who had promised a son to both him and his wife Sarah. But after waiting, now more patiently in response to a further word from a gracious God (Genesis 17:19), Abraham did eventually receive in Isaac the child of promise. God never has anyone greater to swear by and so makes solemn promises by himself. His word through Christ,

---

[xi] James 2:23 'Abraham believed God, and it was reckoned to him as righteousness; and he was called the friend of God.'

[xii] Genesis 16:4 'He slept with Hagar, and she conceived' (NIV).

affirmed by the in-dwelling of his Holy Spirit, is equally to be trusted.

6:16-18 'For men verily swear by the greater, and an oath for confirmation is to them an end of all strife. Wherein God, willing more abundantly to show unto the heirs of promise the immutability of his counsel, confirmed it by an oath, that by two immutable things, in which it was impossible for God to lie, we might have a strong consolation, who have fled for refuge to lay hold upon the hope set before us.'

A man's oath was taken as a sign of binding solemnity and truth, in which his whole nature and character was bound. The unchanging nature of God's promises, made 'Yes and Amen' in Christ ('For all the promises of God in him are 'Yes', and in him 'Amen', to the glory of God through us' - 2 Corinthians 1:20, NKJV), are confirmed to us by two unchangeable things. These are firstly by God's own word, and secondly by God himself - his character - all that God is himself in his nature and all he stands for. There is nothing in the universe greater than these two things. (Psalm 138:2 - 'You have exalted above all things your name and your word.') God's name stands figuratively for all that God is - for God himself; someone for whom lying is an impossibility. God's word is unchanging, and must be received into our hearts for us to get the benefit of it. This does not occur automatically; the Jews that John tells us had in some superficial way believed in Jesus had not done this, and so did not continue with him. John 8:31 and 37: ''Jesus was saying to the Jews who had believed him... I know that you are Abraham's descendants; yet you seek to kill me, because my word has no place in you.''

'Fleeing for refuge' was the legal remedy for someone who had killed a man as a result of an accident. He could escape the 'avenger of blood' (Deuteronomy 19:6-12) from the deceased man's family by fleeing to a designated city and taking hold of the horns of the altar. This is what King David's army commander Joab tried to do to escape the wrath of King Solomon (1 Kings 2:28), but without adequate legal entitlement. Exodus records that the priests poured out the blood of the sacrificial offering there: 'You shall take some of the blood of the bull and put it on the horns of the altar with your finger; and you shall pour out all the blood at the base of the altar.' The shed blood symbolised protection from the avenger. A way has been left open by God himself for us to escape the consequences of our sin, scheduled to receive a similar punishment if left without remedy. All we need to do is to come to Christ and receive from him forgiveness, a free pardon and a new birth. Then we will have laid hold on 'the hope of eternal life' (Titus 1:2).

6:19-20 'This hope we have as an anchor of the soul, a hope both sure and steadfast and one which enters within the veil, where Jesus has entered as a forerunner for us, having become a high priest forever according to the order of Melchizedek.'

The hope of salvation is likened to a great anchor, 'sure' ('***asphalês***' - 'without failing') and steadfast' ('***bebaios***' - 'firm/secure') to safely hold the ship of faith in the storms of life. This confidence, that is itself God's gift to us, allows us to follow Jesus into heaven itself 'beyond the veil'. 'The veil' refers to the curtain of separation that shut men out of the presence of God in the Holy of Holies, which only the High Priest could enter once a year on the Day of Atonement. This is the curtain that was torn in two from top to bottom when Christ died, [xiii] which the Mishnah informs us was a

---

[xiii] Matthew 27:50-51: 'And Jesus cried out again with a loud voice and yielded up his spirit. And behold the veil of the temple was torn in two from top to bottom.'

hands-breadth in thickness. ¹⁸ The tearing symbolises that the way into God's presence has now been opened year-round to all who trust in the sacrifice of Messiah, our forerunner ('***prodomas***' - 'one who comes in advance to a place where the rest are to follow').

The writer then takes us back to Melchizedek, that 'type' (or 'prototype') of Jesus to whose priestly order Jesus has been ordained into by the will of his Father.

Chapter 7

Jesus' eternal priesthood and the guarantee of a better covenant that saves completely.

7:1-3 'For this Melchizedek, king of Salem, priest of the Most High God, who met Abraham as he was returning from the slaughter of the kings and blessed him, to whom also Abraham apportioned a tenth part of all the spoils, was first of all, by the translation of his name, king of righteousness, and then also king of Salem, which is king of peace. Without father, without mother, without genealogy, having neither beginning of days nor end of life, but made like the Son of God, he remains a priest perpetually.'

Back to Melchizedek. God 'Most High' had been worshiped before Abraham was called out of Ur of the Chaldeans (Genesis 11:31) for the long pilgrimage to the land that God promised to his descendants. Melchizedek was, like Jesus, a priestly king whose rule encompasses both peace and righteousness. In tithing to him, Abraham expressed subordination to him and received a blessing (Genesis 14:19). [xiv] Rather like the prophet Elijah, Melchizedek simply appears on the biblical scene then vanishes, leaving us with no record of his earthly ancestry. He can be viewed as a 'type' of Christ (a prophetic forerunner) or even as one of the pre-incarnate appearances of Jesus himself. Like Jesus, God called him to an eternal priesthood. Like Jesus, Melchizedek represents both righteousness ('Christ Jesus, who

---

[xiv] Genesis 14:19-20: 'He blessed him and said, "Blessed be Abram of God Most High, Possessor of heaven and earth; and blessed be God Most High, who has delivered your enemies into your hand." He gave him a tenth of all.'

became to us... righteousness' - 1 Corinthians 1:30) and peace ('A child will be born to us, a son will be given to us... and his name will be called... Prince of Peace' - Isaiah 9:6).

The writer is using a type of rabbinic argument when he connects Melchizedek's unusual absence of recorded genealogy to link him, with Jesus, to an eternal priesthood. In so doing he is establishing Jesus' priestly role (as a non-Levite), after a greater and older order of priests than them, the order of Melchizedek. The rabbis applied four levels of meaning to Scripture in their interpretation of it. Firstly the '***Peshat***' - the 'plain' literal or factual meaning. Secondly there was the '***Remez***' - the 'hints' or allegorical meaning. Thirdly there was the '***Derash***' - the 'inquired' comparative or metaphorical meaning beyond the original context. Finally there was the '***Sod***', which was the 'secret' hidden (but now being revealed) meaning (which was never contrary to or contradictory of the '***Peshat***' meaning). In this way the writer takes the Old Testament text and goes deeper into the meaning to draw out truth in the '***Sod***' form based on what was not stated (such as the absence of genealogy) as well as what was stated. Melchizedek appears as a 'type' of Jesus, a forerunner who has been 'made like' the greater High Priest yet to come.

'Without father and mother' would have been an absolute barrier to participation in the Levitical priesthood, where establishing an acceptable genealogy was a legal requirement. But the writer is able to connect the silence of Genesis 14 in regards to Melchizedek's family with Psalm 110:4 and the eternal priesthood of the Messiah.

7:4-7 'Now observe how great this man was to whom Abraham, the patriarch, gave a tenth of the choicest spoils. And those indeed of the sons of Levi who receive the priest's office have a commandment in the Law to collect a tenth from the people, that is, from their

brethren, although these are descended from Abraham. But the one whose genealogy is not traced from them collected a tenth from Abraham and blessed the one who had the promises. But without any dispute the lesser is blessed by the greater.'

The writer reminds his Jewish audience that the greatest of their patriarchs paid tithes (a clear sign of inferiority) and was blessed (again a sign in that culture of a senior person) by a man who was not of the same family and lineage. Melchizedek's priestly ministry on behalf of the God whom Abraham served had begun in all likelihood long before God called Abraham out of Ur. As such Melchizedek was therefore an important priest in the plan of God long before the Aaronic and Levitical priesthood was established. The tithe was paid in 'the valley of Shaveh' (Genesis 14:17) - 'the king's valley', a likely reference to Melchizedek, the king of Salem, who comes there to meet Abraham (at that point called 'Abram') and bless him.

7:8-10 'In this case mortal men receive tithes, but in that case one receives them, of whom it is witnessed that he lives on. And, so to speak, through Abraham even Levi, who received tithes, paid tithes, for he was still in the loins of his father when Melchizedek met him.'

Jesus was not physically descended from the priestly tribe of Aaron and Levi. The writer quotes the clearly messianic prophecy of Psalm 110:4 ('The Lord has sworn and will not change his mind, "You are a priest forever, according to the order of Melchizedek"') to support his argument that Jesus is a messianic priest despite being from Judah, a non-priestly tribe. The order of Melchizedek is shown by the Psalm to have perpetual effect, hence Melchizedek lived on, at least in as far as his ministry was concerned. His greatness could be seen by the fact that even Levi, the as yet unborn descendent of Jacob, paid tithes to him through his forefather Abraham.

7:11 'Now if perfection was through the Levitical priesthood (for on the basis of it the people received the Law), what further need was there for another priest to arise according to the order of Melchizedek, and not be designated according to the order of Aaron?'

Deep down every religious Jew knew that their beloved Torah was powerless to change the attitudes of their hearts. It could and did regulate their behaviour in a way that was legally acceptable to God, but as the Apostle Paul commented, it was powerless to bring about the inner change that God was also looking for. 'What the law was powerless to do in that it was weakened by the sinful nature, God did by sending his own Son' - Romans 8:3 (NIV). So 'perfection' was not actually possible under the reign of the Law, good and of God though the Law was. Jesus himself upheld the Law - "Which one of you convicts me of sin?" (John 8:46). What he condemned was the prevailing attitude of the men who taught it ("Woe to you, Scribes and Pharisees, hypocrites...' - Matthew 23:13-36).

The Law, Paul tells us in Galatians 3:24, was a type of legal guardian or tutor necessary to teach us the standards and requirements of a holy God, and so bring us to the point of recognising our need to be saved and the futility of our own efforts alone in bringing this about. The Law convicted and convinced us of our sinfulness but was powerless to help us keep the Law; it acts as a kind of tutor or law enforcer, not as a social-worker. Inner change was only possible through the sort of faith Abraham demonstrated when he 'believed God and it was reckoned to him as righteousness' (Genesis 15:6). The priesthood of this type of saving faith was inaugurated by the person of Melchizedek.

7:12-14 'For when the priesthood is changed, of necessity there takes place a change of law also. For the one concerning whom these things are spoken belongs to another tribe, from which no one has officiated at the altar. For it is evident that our Lord was descended from Judah, a tribe with reference to which Moses spoke nothing concerning priests.'

The 'law' that the writer has in mind here is the sacrificial law associated with the purpose and functioning of the Levitical priesthood. The writer is not referring to the moral law, which was established through Moses in the Ten Commandments before the Levitical priesthood had come into being. God has no intention of changing his moral standards. But the law governing the sacrifices and offerings of the priests would necessarily have to change if the priesthood changed, to accommodate and reflect the nature and activity of the new priesthood. The priesthood of Melchizedek was also prior to the Law of Moses being given, and any law associated with it is not bound to or encumbered in any way by the many rules governing the work of the Levites. The fact that Jesus was not descended from a priestly family (although his mother Mary was) [19] suddenly becomes irrelevant as an obstacle to a Jew placing their faith in him. Melchizedek existed long before the tribes of Israel came into being. In pre-dating them he is not bound to any of them, and neither is Christ, who as an eternal member of the Godhead pre-dated them all. Instead, Christ fulfils the many prophecies that stated that Messiah would be a descendant of David, of Judah's lineage. For example, 'The sceptre shall not depart from Judah, nor the ruler's staff from between his feet, until Shiloh comes, and to him shall be the obedience of the peoples' (Genesis 49:10).

7:15-17 'And this is clearer still, if another priest arises according to the likeness of Melchizedek, who has become such not on the basis of a law of physical requirement, but according to the power of an indestructible life. For it is attested of him, "You are a priest forever according to the order of Melchizedek."'

Jesus' priestly ministry, being of the order of Melchizedek, is from an altogether older and superior order of priests, and free of the need to be associated with Aaron's and Levi's. The Levitical priesthood served to disempower people within a hierarchy at the top of which in human terms was the High Priest. Melchizedek's blessing (made prophetically with bread and wine as in Jesus' sacrifice) over Abraham empowered in him boldness and spiritual insight that enabled him to say to the King of Sodom (Genesis 14:22-24), 'I have sworn to the Lord God Most High, possessor of heaven and earth, that I will not take a thread or a sandal thong or anything that is yours, for fear you would say, 'I have made Abram rich'.'

The ministry of Melchizedek empowered and gave authority, just as the ministry of Jesus does. Jesus' 'likeness' to Melchizedek is based on his kingship in a place where peace and righteousness are two of the ruling characteristics (Hebrews 7:2). Jesus' 'indestructible life' (death could not hold him) is perfectly placed to complement the eternal priesthood that Psalm 110:4 speaks of. Jesus' eternal nature within the Godhead allows him to perfectly fulfil the qualification of Messiah to be 'a priest forever'.

7:18-22 'For on the one hand, there is a setting aside of a former commandment because of its weakness and uselessness, (for the Law made nothing perfect), and on the other hand there is a bringing in of a better hope, through which we draw near to God. And inasmuch as it was not without an oath (for they indeed became priests without an oath, but he with an oath through the One who said to him, 'The Lord has sworn and will not change his mind, "You are a priest forever"'), so much the more also Jesus has become the guarantee of a better covenant.'

Once again the Law of Moses' powerlessness to save or even to produce any lasting positive change in the heart of man is held up as evidence of the need for a spiritual change. The Law in fact had the contrary effect - knowledge of it awoke and provoked latent rebellious and sinful desires. 'I would not have come to know sin except through the Law; for I would not have known about coveting if the Law had not said 'You shall not covet' (Romans 7:7). The Law informed man's sinful nature as to what God prohibited, and so gave sin a focal point to direct its rebellion. The change in priesthood through the sacrifice Christ made of himself brought with it a much 'better hope'. Through this hope and confidence we can draw near to God to find grace and help (Hebrews 4:16), and have him draw near to us. (Draw near to God and he will draw near to you' - James 4:8.)

The sworn promise ('oath') of God's found in Psalm 110 verse 4 has now been fulfilled by the One that so many of the Psalms were written to speak about. He has been given a better priesthood, with a better sacrifice and a better law. 'The law of the Spirit of life in Christ Jesus has set you free from the law of sin and of death' (Romans 8:2). It is not hard to see why Jesus is the mediator of a much, much 'better covenant' relationship with Father God.

7:23-25 'The former priests, on the one hand, existed in greater numbers because they were prevented by death from continuing, but Jesus, on the other hand, because he continues forever, holds his priesthood permanently. Therefore he is able also to save forever those who draw near to God through him, since he always lives to make intercession for them.'

The Levites were subject to the same laws of mortality as any other human being. Being limited in time and place and their inability to do more than one thing at a time they were subject to the same restrictions as any other human institution. Jesus' resurrected life, on the other hand, means that he is subject to none of these restrictions and so can meet all needs simultaneously from a position outside the bounds of time. Melchizedek's unending priesthood perfectly matches Jesus' eternal nature. Jesus' priestly intercessory prayer for our salvation is efficacious because it is totally pure, totally powerful and continues outside of time ungoverned by any restrictive factors and under the rule of grace and mercy. What a Saviour!

7:26-28 'For it was fitting for us to have such a high priest, holy, innocent, undefiled, separated from sinners and exalted above the heavens; who does not need daily, like those high priests, to offer up sacrifices, first for his own sins and then for the sins of the people, because this he did once for all when he offered up himself. For the Law appoints men as high priests who are weak, but the word of the oath, which came after the Law, appoints a Son, made perfect forever.'

Being men, the high priests were far from being holy, innocent and undefiled. Their family (under Annas) at the time of Christ was notorious for their 'get rich quick' religion based on extortion. Worshippers' money had to be changed at high rates into the 'pure' Temple coins needed to purchase the legally guaranteed 'clean' animals for sacrifice. Then further extortionate prices were levied at their sale. Jesus (Matthew 21:12-14) was not the only Jewish scholar to object to this practice. The Mishnah (Kerithuth 1:7) tells of a first century Rabbi, Simeon ben Gamaliel, who successfully countered the extortionate sums demanded for the sacrificial doves required for the purification of women following childbirth.

The priests also kept themselves separate from the common or garden unlearned 'sinners' ('This crowd which does not know the Law is accursed' - John 7:49), and from a sense of despising such people rather than from a desire to keep themselves pure for God's service. Before making the offering on behalf of the people the High Priest had to offer a sacrifice for his own sins. The 'oath' of Psalm 110 verse 4 (made after the moral and sacrificial law was given) that the priestly office of Melchizedek would be eternal, is fulfilled in the eternal person of Messiah, the only person without sin and therefore qualified to act as both priest and sacrifice simultaneously.

Jesus' incarnation and subsequent suffering and death 'finished' the mission that his Father had given him to accomplish. He was made 'perfect' through that process of suffering (Hebrews 2:10) in the sense of being the mature finished article of model sonship. Jesus could also offer his sacrifice as a 'perfect' Son in the sense of the completeness that he brought to the role, as God become man, for that specific sacrificial purpose.

Chapter 8

Jesus - a more excellent ministry; the mediator of a better covenant

8:1-3 'Now the main point in what has been said is this: we have such a high priest, who has taken his seat at the right hand of the throne of the Majesty in the heavens, a minister in the sanctuary and in the true tabernacle, which the Lord pitched, not man. For every high priest is appointed to offer both gifts and sacrifices, so it is necessary that this high priest also have something to offer.'

Jesus' seat at his Father's right hand designates his authority to rule and judge on his Father's behalf, indeed the Father has placed all such tasks (e.g. authority - Matthew 28:18, and judgement - John 5:22) in the care of his beloved only begotten Son. The 'true tabernacle' referred to is the one set up in heaven, of which the earthly tabernacle and later the Temple were but crude copies. Heaven has been 'pitched' ('*pêgnumi*' - 'To build or fix something by fastening it together') by God himself, the architect and creator of the universe. The 'true tabernacle' of verse 2 describes God's dwelling in heaven. Psalm 104:2 describes God in creation, 'Stretching out the heavens like a tent (*tabernacle*) curtain', and God further revealed himself in the incarnate tabernacle of the Lord Jesus Christ. John (1:14) describes this as: 'The Word became flesh and tabernacled among us' - a 'tabernacle' that became a sacrifice for our sin. Jesus has something much more special to offer than anything any of the high priests on earth had access to - the offering of his own blood. These 'tabernacle' illustrations underline God's desire to make fellowship with man possible. God's revelation of himself towards mankind is a dynamic process that Amos prophesied would include re-building the tabernacle of David, [xv] something that James reminded the early church council in Jerusalem of (Acts 15:16-18), in regard to God providing access to his presence to the Gentiles. This amazing access and inclusion of others is a dynamic one for each generation of God's people to wrestle with as they seek to make the way to peace with God known through evangelism. It will culminate with 'a tabernacle of testimony in heaven being opened' (Revelation 15:5). As such God's name 'I am' incorporates an unfolding of his own unchanging nature for his people to be joined to, through the sacrifice of Christ on the cross.

8:4-6 'Now if he were on earth, he would not be a priest at all, since there are those who offer the gifts according to the Law; who serve a copy and shadow of the heavenly things, just as Moses was warned by God when he was about to erect the tabernacle, for, "See", he says, "that you make all things according to the pattern which was shown you on the mountain." But now he has obtained a more excellent ministry, by as much as he is also the mediator of a better covenant, which has been enacted on better promises.'

Jesus was not a member of the Levitical priesthood; rather he was from the tribe of Judah. Like Moses, he was highly educated, being addressed both as '***Rhabbi***' (Rabbi) and '***Didaskalôs***' ('Doctor' of Torah). Consequently he did not serve in the Temple as a priest, but rather taught Torah in the Court of Israel, just as he had taught Torah to Moses on Mount Sinai. Devout Jews such as Mary and Joseph would have followed the Law's injunction to train their son to the level of his ability in Torah. As part of the rabbinic system Jesus

---

[xv] Amos 9:11 'In that day I will raise up the fallen booth of David, and wall up its breaches; I will also raise up its ruins, and rebuild it as in the days of old.'

would have then graduated at age 30 from the company of the Doctors of Law that he had so impressed with his genius for Torah at age 12 (Luke 2:47). [xvi] Jesus' father Joseph had in all likelihood served as a '*tekton*' in the construction of the Temple of Herod, which had required 10,000 Jewish craftsmen. Some of these had to train the 1000 priests as builders and '*tektons*', the skills Josephus documents as needed to build the 135 feet tall Holy Place within the existing Court of the Priests. [20] The task of training the elitist class of priests would have fallen to devout Jewish '*tektons*', of which Joseph is one of the few known historic examples.

As an educated person and a '*tekton*' builder by profession Jesus is therefore readily comparable with Moses who was required to build the first dwelling-place of God in the form of the tabernacle. Moses (as Solomon was to do later) copied the pattern ('plan') shown to him on Mount Sinai by none other than the pre-incarnate Jesus himself. The passage being quoted here is Exodus 25:40; [xvii] and 'pattern' is '*tabnith*' - 'a plan for a construction or structure'. [21] As Stephen said to the Sanhedrin, "Our fathers had the tabernacle of testimony in the wilderness, just as he who spoke to Moses directed him to make it according to the pattern which he had seen" (Acts 7:44).

The 'pattern' for the tabernacle shown by God to Moses became the plans upon which the construction drawings for the temple of Solomon and Herod were based. Jesus was born into a family of Jewish '*tektons*'; Joseph could explain the Temple plans to the

---

[xvi] Luke 2:46-47 'After three days they found him in the temple, sitting in the midst of the teachers, both listening to them and asking them questions. And all who heard him were amazed at his understanding and his answers.

[xvii] Exodus 25:40 'See that you make them after the pattern for them, which was shown to you on the mountain.'

priests (whose job it was to do the actual building work on the Holy Place within the Court of the Priests) and oversee them in their work as a master tekton ('***architekton***'). This is the exact term that the Apostle Paul, a tentmaker, uses of his own ministry (1 Corinthians 3:10). [xviii]

Jesus' ministry is then once again favourably compared to that of Moses. In verse 8, the word used for 'enacting' the better promises in the legal agreement inaugurated by Christ's new covenant is in fact '***nomotheteô***', the same term used in Hebrews 7:11 for 'receiving the Law', as Moses had on Mount Sinai. The one who appeared to Moses and gave him Torah has now completed the giving of Torah through the sacrifice of himself at Calvary, only with much 'better promises' that the in-dwelling of the Holy Spirit brings. This puts the words of the New Covenant in the same category as Torah to the writer's Jewish audience in terms of divine revelation, only with much greater impact and importance. The 'better promises' of this covenant's 'new Torah' include the outpouring of the Spirit and the promise of everlasting life to all who put their trust in Jesus. As Paul told the church in Rome, 'The law of the Spirit of life in Christ Jesus has set you free from the law of sin and of death' (Romans 8:2).

8:7-9 'For if that first covenant had been faultless, there would have been no occasion sought for a second. For finding fault with them, he says, "Behold, the days are coming, says the Lord, when I will effect a new covenant with the house of Israel and with the house of Judah. Not like the covenant which I made with their fathers on the day when I took them by the hand to lead them out of the

---

[xviii] 1 Corinthians 3:10 'According to the grace of God which was given to me, like a wise master-builder ('***architekton***') I laid a foundation, and another is building on it.'

land of Egypt; for they did not continue in my covenant and I did not care for them, says the Lord."'

The first covenant was based on the law given to Moses, and man's inability to keep that law rendered the covenant faulty. One of the main purposes of the law was to show sinful and proud men and women that they could not in their own strength keep God's righteous requirements, and so were in desperate need of a saviour. The second covenant was clearly foretold by the prophet Jeremiah, to whom the writer now appeals to further back up, from the Jewish scriptures, the points he is making regarding the 'better' covenant that Messiah's sacrificial death had inaugurated. God the Father had led his people tenderly by the hand out of Egypt and into the Promised Land. As Hosea related (11:3-4): 'It is I who taught Ephraim to walk, I took them in my arms; but they did not know that I healed them. I led them with cords of a man, with bonds of love.' Their rejection of him in pursuit of the pagan gods of the surrounding nations caused God in great pain to discipline them, as any loving father would, and to foretell through Jeremiah the coming (new) Covenant that would have the power of the Spirit to bring about an internal change of disposition towards God.

Jeremiah 31:32-34 reads: 'Behold, the days are coming, declares the Lord, when I will make a new covenant with the house of Israel, and with the house of Judah; not like the covenant that I made with their fathers in the day that I took them by the hand to bring them out of the land of Egypt; my covenant which they broke, although I was a husband to them, says the Lord. But this shall be the covenant that I will make with the house of Israel after those days, declares the Lord, "I will put my law within them and on their heart I will write it; and I will be their God, and they shall be my people. They will not teach again, each man his neighbour and each man his brother, saying, "Know the Lord," for they will all know me, from the least of them to the greatest of them," declares the Lord, "for I will forgive their iniquity, and their sin I will remember no more."'

The Lord did not 'care' for the people who rejected him; not in the sense of not loving them but rather in the sense of a calculated neglect - care here is '***ameleô***' meaning 'to neglect'. [22] The people of Israel, in their rebellious and sinful behaviour, ran into the terrible consequences of their disobedience described in Deuteronomy 28:15-68. (E.g. verses 63 and 64: 'The Lord will delight over you to make you perish and destroy you; and you will be torn from the land where you are entering to possess it. Moreover, the Lord will scatter you among all peoples, from one end of the earth to the other end of the earth.') The people's rejection of God brought upon themselves ever increasing cycles of discipline, with the intended purpose of turning them back to him.

8:10-13 'For this is the covenant that I will make with the house of Israel after those days, says the Lord. I will put my laws into their minds, and I will write them on their hearts. I will be their God, and they shall be my people. And they shall not teach everyone his fellow citizen, saying, "Know the Lord," for all will know me, from the least to the greatest of them. For I will be merciful to their iniquities, and I will remember their sins no more.' When he said, "A new covenant," he has made the first obsolete. But whatever is becoming obsolete and growing old is ready to disappear.'

Continuing with the prophecy of Jeremiah, the writer points out that the indwelling Spirit provides a much more efficacious 'heart' treatment by bringing us into true relationship with God. 'Know' the Lord is '***ginôskô***', meaning 'to come to know and be acquainted with'. This relational dynamic grows through prayer, meditation and worship of a God who fully knows us, and never stops loving us, flawed though we are. The New Covenant opens the way to know God in the same way that he knows us. 1 Corinthians 13:12: 'Now we see in a mirror dimly, but then face to face; now I know in part, but then I will know fully just as I also have been fully known.' God promises that we shall know him as fully as he knows us, and that in the continual unveiling of all the limitless grace, power and glory of God throughout eternity, we shall fully know as we are fully known.

This new relationship-based covenant of in-dwelling makes the old covenant redundant ('obsolete' is ***palaioô***' - 'to decay and wear out') and 'ready to disappear' once all the Old Testament prophecies concerning it are fulfilled. In the meantime 'We all with unveiled face, beholding as in a mirror the glory of the Lord, are being transformed into the same image from glory to glory, just as from the Lord, the Spirit' (2 Corinthians 3:18). This is a work which moves towards receiving a new body in heaven, thus completing the salvation process.

Chapter 9

Jesus - offered once to bear the sins of many

9:1-2 'Now even the first covenant had regulations of divine worship and the earthly sanctuary. For there was a tabernacle prepared, the outer one, in which were the lampstand and the table and the sacred bread; this is called the holy place.'

The covenant God made with the people of Israel was governed by the Law's instructions on how God wanted the sacrifices to be made, how his people were to live and how they were to approach him. It was developed as a model of the worship of heaven, but with built-in limitations necessary given the fact that it was a replica made on earth by men, and also to show that the actual fullness of what 'right relationship' ('righteousness') with God entailed had yet to come. The items contained within the outer part of the tent (the Holy Place) were intended to communicate spiritual truth to the people and remind them of their spiritual heritage, founded on their selection by God himself, based on their lowly position. [xix] From this God would bring glory to his own name through his merciful dealing with them in making a covenant with them.

The lampstand was made as instructed in Exodus 25:31-36: 'Then you shall make a lampstand of pure gold... of hammered work; its cups, its bulbs and its flowers shall be of one piece with it. Six branches shall go out from its sides; three branches of the lampstand from its one side and three branches of the lampstand from its other

---

[xix] Deuteronomy 7:7 'The Lord did not set his love on you nor choose you because you were more in number than any of the peoples, for you were the fewest of all peoples.'

side. Three cups shall be shaped like almond blossoms in the one branch, a bulb and a flower... so for six branches going out from the lampstand; and in the lampstand four cups shaped like almond blossoms, its bulbs and its flowers. A bulb shall be under the first pair of branches coming out of it, and a bulb under the second pair of branches coming out of it, and a bulb under the third pair of branches coming out of it, for the six branches coming out of the lampstand. Their bulbs and their branches shall be of one piece with it; all of it shall be one piece of hammered work of pure gold.' The lamp was inclined westward towards the Most Holy Place, and was lit by fire from the altar of incense. [23] The Arch of Titus in Rome (excerpt shown below) depicts both the candlestick (Menorah) and the table of the showbread in the hands of the victorious Roman army.

The lamp represents Jesus, the light of the world. The heavenly city of Revelation 21:23 needs no sun or moon because the Lamb (Jesus) is its light. Like Jesus, his people are also to be 'the light of the world' (Matthew 5:14). Once a person receives the Holy Spirit, they share in Jesus' own nature and are one with him, just as the different branches of the lamp are all of the same material (pure gold) and hammered from one piece, thus symbolising both purity and unity.

The table that held the showbread was also made to the prescribed design: 'You shall make a table of acacia wood, two cubits long and one cubit wide and one and a half cubits high. You shall overlay it with pure gold and make a gold border around it. You shall make for it a rim of a handbreadth around it; and you shall make a gold border for the rim around it. You shall make four gold rings for it and put rings on the four corners which are on its four feet. The rings shall be close to the rim as holders for the poles to carry the table' (Exodus 25:23-27). The table and the lamp are depicted on the Arch of Titus in Rome, having been removed by him following the Roman siege of Jerusalem in AD 70. The table's feet were turned out and shaped to represent those of animals, and the legs connected by a golden plate, which was surrounded by a 'crown,' or wreath, while another wreath ran round the top of the table. [24]

The 'sacred bread' was 'the bread of the presence' ('showbread'), set before God's 'face'. The Hebrew here is '***lechem panim***', literally meaning 'bread before' or 'the bread of faces' They were marked with priestly frankincense (Leviticus 24:7), hence pointed towards the priestly role that Messiah, 'the bread of life', would have (John 6:35). These twelve pieces of unleavened bread, standing for the twelve tribes were eaten by the priests following the baking of a replacement batch every Sabbath day. It was this bread that Ahimelech the priest gave to David and his companions to eat (1 Samuel 21:2). The weekly process of changing the 'showbread' is described in the Mishnah (*Menahot xi. 7*): 'Four priests enter (the Holy Place), two carrying (*each*) one of the piles (*of six showbread*), the other two the two dishes (*of incense*). Four priests preceded them, two to take off the two (*old*) piles of showbread, and two the two (*old*) dishes of incense. Those who brought in (*the bread and* *incense*) stood at the north side (*of the table*), facing southwards... as it is written: "Thou shalt set upon the table bread of the Presence before me always"' (Exodus 25:30, *words in italics are mine*). [25]

9:3-5 'Behind the second veil there was a tabernacle which is called the Holy of Holies, having a golden censer and the ark of the covenant covered on all sides with gold, in which was a golden jar holding the manna, and Aaron's rod which budded, and the tables of the covenant; and above it were the cherubim of glory overshadowing the mercy seat; but of these things we cannot now speak in detail.'

The altar of incense was located in the Holy Place (not in the Holy of Holies), and the priests offered incense there by lot twice daily. It was there that Zechariah was offering incense when he found himself face-to-face with the angel Gabriel, who announced the news of the coming birth of his son John the Baptist (Luke 1:8-17). Once a year, on the Day of Atonement, the High Priest would take coals from the altar with incense and also bull's blood to offer in the Holy of Holies (Leviticus 16:12-14). [xx]

The inner part of the tabernacle ('tent of meeting') was divided from the outer by a curtain (the second veil). Within was the altar (the 'mercy seat' - '*hilastêrion*' - the cover of the ark of the covenant), where, once a year on the Day of Atonement, the High Priest would

---

[xx] Leviticus 16:12-14 'He shall take a censer full of coals of fire from upon the altar before the Lord and two handfuls, of finely ground sweet incense, and bring it inside the veil. He shall put the incense on the fire before the Lord, that the cloud of incense may cover the mercy seat that is on the ark of the testimony, otherwise he will die. Moreover, he shall take some of the blood of the bull and sprinkle it with his finger on the mercy seat on the east side; also in front of the mercy seat he shall sprinkle some of the blood with his finger seven times.'

sprinkle animal blood to represent the cleansing of the sin of the people that the animal's sacrificial death was for. God had taken the initiative in providing a solution for the problem of the sin of mankind interfering with relationship with him. This sacrificial act allowed God's just wrath against sin to be 'propitiated' on his terms (*'hilaskomai'* - 'expiated'), the word from which 'mercy seat' is derived. It was not man appeasing God; rather it was God providing a way for his holiness and justice to be reconciled in the midst of the problem of man's sin, at a place where God's grace and mercy met efficaciously on behalf of sinful man. As such the 'mercy seat' represents an Old Covenant prefigurement of 'the throne of grace' that the writer has described in chapter 4 verse 16, the place where we find 'grace to help us in our time of need', in other words help above and beyond simply being forgiven. God does more than simply forgive, he pours out on us heaven's riches so that we may have all the strength we need to become all he desires us being.

Within the Holy of Holies of the Tabernacle (it is believed to have been lost at the time of the exile to Babylon c. 597 BC) was the 'ark', the sacred box carried on poles and containing items from Israel's history denoting God's particular involvement with them. These were the stone tablets inscribed with the commandments that Moses had received on Mount Sinai from the pre-incarnate person of the Lord Jesus Christ, the eternal second person of the triune Godhead. There was a golden jar containing the bread with which God had fed his people during the 40 years in the desert wilderness, maintained as a testimony to them both of God's supernatural provision for them and at the same time of their underlying unbelief. ('Manna' means 'What is it?') [26] The people had refused to trust in God's on-going provision and had hoarded it for the following day; it had grown mouldy (Exodus 16:20) and they had been rebuked for their lack of trust in God's provision.

Aaron's tribe had been selected from the people of Israel, witnessed to by the miraculous budding of the stick of almond-tree wood that he carried; it had not only budded but had actually grown almonds overnight (Exodus 17:8). The altar was overshadowed by two carved and gold-covered figures of angels ('cherubim'), symbolising a meeting-place with a holy God: 'There I will meet with you; and from above the mercy seat, from between the two cherubim which are upon the ark of the testimony, I will speak to you about all that I will give you in commandment for the sons of Israel' (Exodus 25:22). Images of cherubim were woven into the curtain of the Tabernacle - the place of meeting (Exodus 26:1). Psalm 80:1 and Psalm 99:1 make it clear that the God of Israel sits enthroned between angelic beings called cherubim. They accompany the throne of God in the vision of the prophet Ezekiel (Ezekiel 10:20 'These are the living beings that I saw beneath the God of Israel by the river Chebar; so I knew that they were cherubim').

The writer knows that his audience is familiar with the significance of these items and is restricted in the amount of time and space he can devote to them (fortunately these limitations do not apply now). They are all shadows ('types') of God's gracious provision to his people, and of Christ himself - 'Although Christ be but one, yet he is understood by us under a variety of forms. He is the Tabernacle, on account of the human body in which he dwelt. He is the Table, because he is our Bread of life. He is the Ark which has the law of God enclosed within, because he is the Word of the Father. He is the Candlestick, because he is our spiritual light. He is the Altar of incense, because he is the sweet-smelling odour of sanctification. He is the Altar of burnt-offering, because he is the victim, by death on the cross, for the sins of the whole world.' [27]

9:6-7 'Now when these things have been so prepared, the priests are continually entering the outer tabernacle performing the divine worship, but into the second only

the high priest enters once a year, not without taking blood, which he offers for himself and for the sins of the people committed in ignorance.'

The sacrifices and offerings that the priests made on a daily basis were a form of worship, one that God had commanded, but which were location specific (the tabernacle) and person specific - only those from a priestly family could participate in making them. The new covenant inaugurated in Christ's own blood means that all men and women who are members by faith of his covenant family can enter, through the Holy Spirit, into his very presence in heaven. This is the real Holy of Holies, where they can offer a worshipful sacrifice of praise and thanks. For as David had prophetically prayed, 'Sacrifice and meal offering you have not desired; my ears you have opened; burnt offering and sin offering you have not required. Then I said, "Behold, I come; in the scroll of the book it is written of me. I delight to do your will, O my God; your Law is within my heart" (Psalms 40:6-8). God was interested in the heart-sourced Spirit-led worship from all of his people, not simply from a sub-set of Priests. The prophet Hosea (6:6) reinforced this: 'I delight in loyalty rather than sacrifice, and in the knowledge of God rather than burnt offerings.'

Once again the writer unfavourably compares that greatest of Israelite priests, the High Priest, with the person and ministry of the Lord Jesus Christ. The High Priest has sins of his own to atone for; Christ was without sin. The High Priest offered a sacrifice only once a year; Christ stands always in his Father's presence making intercession for us (Romans 8:34). Christ offers his own blood, that of the sinless Son of God, whereas the High Priest's offering was that of an animal. The High Priest entered a tent, Christ entered heaven itself.

'Ignorance' here is '***agnoêma***' - 'without understanding'. The Jews were not ignorant of God's righteous requirements; they were very well versed in Torah and most did their best to keep it and attain, with the Apostle Paul, to the 'righteousness of their own derived from the Law' (Philippians 3:9). 'Sins committed in ignorance' here refers to ignorance of the true and ultimate way to please God that the writer is describing, that is, through faith and trust in the once-and-for-all offering of himself that Jesus made on our behalf on the cross. God is well-aware of our limitations in our grasping of his ways and has, in Jesus' sacrifice, made provision for this as well as for our other sins.

9:8-10: 'The Holy Spirit is signifying this, that the way into the holy place has not yet been disclosed while the outer tabernacle is still standing, which is a symbol for the present time. Accordingly both gifts and sacrifices are offered which cannot make the worshiper perfect in conscience, since they relate only to food and drink and various washings, regulations for the body imposed until a time of reformation.'

The passage as shown is one of two ways of rendering of the Greek text. Verse 8 reads literally that 'the holiest way was not manifested while the first tabernacle was standing'. The 'way' ('***hodos***') does indeed denote a path or access route; it is also one of the titles the Lord Jesus used of himself (John 14:6 - 'I am the way, the truth and the life'). That person of 'the way', and the amazing consequences of his sacrifice in terms of access to God's presence, had indeed 'not been disclosed' ('***phaneroô***' - 'to make manifest or visible or known what has been hidden or unknown') while the tent of meeting stood.

Jesus was made manifest in the flesh while the Temple (not the Tabernacle) stood. As previously stated his earthly father Joseph would have been one of a very few devout Jewish '***tektons***' at that time (18 BC) and place (Judea) qualified and able to instruct the Jewish priests needed to do the actual work of building. [28] 'Symbol' here is '***parabolê***' ('placing of one thing by the side of another for the purpose of comparison' or 'parable' as in the teaching illustrations that Jesus gave), [29] a picture of something greater and eternal that the earthly model was intended to communicate. At the time of writing ('the present time' - verse 9), the Temple had yet to be destroyed. The earthly model was still standing in Temple form, however in just a few years it would be destroyed in fulfilment of Jesus' prophecy (Matthew 24:1-2). [xxi]

All Jews knew that their outward legal observances did nothing to change their fundamental inner dispositions; their consciences (verse 9) were not yet perfected. The Law was powerless to help in that regard, 'For what the Law could not do, weak as it was through the flesh, God did, sending his own Son in the likeness of sinful flesh and as an offering for sin' (Romans 8:3). In Jesus, 'reformation' ('***diorthôsis***' - 'to make straight') had arrived. No longer were the minutiae of the Law required in respect to 'Food and drink and various washings', rather, 'all was declared clean' (Mark 7:9).

Israel's prophets had pointed the people towards this 'time of reformation'. "Behold, days are coming," declares the Lord, "when I will make a new covenant with the house of Israel and with the house of Judah, not like the covenant which I made with their fathers in the day I took them by the hand to bring them out of the land of Egypt, my covenant which they broke, although I was a husband to them," declares the Lord. "But this is the covenant which I will make with the house of Israel after those days," declares the Lord, "I will put

---

[xxi] Matthew 24:1-2 'His disciples came up to point out the temple buildings to him. And he said to them, "Do you not see all these things? Truly I say to you, not one stone here will be left upon another, which will not be torn down."'

my law within them and on their heart I will write it; and I will be their God, and they shall be my people. They will not teach again, each man his neighbour and each man his brother, saying, 'Know the Lord,' for they will all know me, from the least of them to the greatest of them," declares the Lord, "for I will forgive their iniquity, and their sin I will remember no more" (Jeremiah 31:31-34). Through the prophet God reveals the passion of his heart - that ordinary people unqualified for this privilege except by the determined grace of God will actually come into relationship with him and they will know him.

A new and much better covenant was coming, one not based on man's ability or otherwise to keep the Law, with failure 'covered' by animal blood-sacrifice, but with the Holy Spirit writing his Law inside men and women's hearts, and the problem of sin dealt with by the most perfect sacrifice of all. Upon Jesus' death, the curtain that blocked the access to the Holy of Holies was torn in two, from top to bottom (Matthew 27:51), indicating that God, and not man, was responsible for permanently opening the way into his presence.

9:11-12 'But when Christ appeared as a high priest of the good things to come, he entered through the greater and more perfect tabernacle not made with hands, that is to say, not of this creation; and not through the blood of goats and calves, but through his own blood he entered the holy place once for all, having obtained eternal redemption.'

The ultimate High Priest, Jesus of Nazareth, entered the 'greater' eternal place of meeting that is heaven itself, with an atoning offering of his own precious blood. The redemption ('ransom') won is a much greater one than the single years worth that the shed blood of the sacrificial animals achieved; Jesus' sacrifice won an eternal redemption. Jesus' blood was poured out before his Father in heaven, the true Holy of Holies, as a completely acceptable and perfect sacrifice for the sin of all humanity across all time. Every single atoning offering in the centuries before Jesus was as it were a further gracious credit by God, which meant that Israel on behalf of all humanity was accruing a huge debt. Every one of the sacrifices in the tabernacle and then in the Temple pointed forward to the moment when those being temporarily pardoned would be made complete eternally. In that sense, Jesus entry into heaven with his own blood is the very centre of history. All the sins of humanity before that day fly forward to be included in his sacrifice. Ever since then, every sin is linked backwards in history to that moment. His redemption for us is complete and, as the writer says, 'eternal'.

9:13-14 'For if the blood of goats and bulls and the ashes of a heifer sprinkling those who have been defiled sanctify for the cleansing of the flesh, how much more will the blood of Christ, who through the eternal Spirit offered himself without blemish to God, cleanse your conscience from dead works to serve the living God?'

This rhetorical question is a typically rabbinic New Testament one. How much more? How much better is Jesus' sacrifice than the sacrifice of an animal? How much more efficacious was the atonement won by Jesus' own blood, over the blood of an animal? Infinitely more! There is no comparison; that is the point of the question. Our conscience (*'suneidêsis'* - 'a knowing with', i.e. 'a co-knowledge with oneself') [30] is cleansed by faith in Jesus' sacrifice from the 'dead' (repetitive and unfruitful) works of our own efforts into 'good works', prepared by God the Father himself for us to walk into. 'We are his workmanship, created in Christ Jesus for good works, which God prepared beforehand so that we would walk in them' (Ephesians 2:10).

9:15-17 'For this reason he is the mediator of a new covenant, so that, since a death has taken place for the redemption of the transgressions that were committed under the first covenant, those who have been called may receive the promise of the eternal inheritance. For where a covenant is, there must of necessity be the death of the one who made it. For a covenant is valid only when men are dead, for it is never in force while the one who made it lives.'

Jesus is our 'mediator' or 'arbitrator'. The Greek here is '***mesitês***', from '***mesos***' meaning 'middle'. Jesus is truly the 'middle-man' between God and humankind, someone who (being both fully God and fully man) can perfectly represent both God and man in the same person. The last will and testament (literally 'covenant') of an individual could only be put into action when the person died. And so God became man in the second person of the Godhead so that as a man he might die bodily in our place. As Paul says (1 Timothy 2:5) 'For there is one God and one mediator between God and men, the man Christ Jesus.' The crucial phrase there is 'the man'. Only as a man could Jesus, the Son of God die and not only pay the price for our redemption but also release to us the inheritance that could only come after his death.

The writer uses the violent death and consequential shedding of Jesus' blood to illustrate his point that the old covenant has been completed with the death of the one who appeared to Abraham to make it in the first place (Genesis 15). There is now a new covenant in place, one founded on the 'better promises' (Hebrews 8:6). We have an eternal inheritance as a result of participating in the new covenant, one that admits us into God's own family household based on adoptive familial ties that lead to voluntary service based on the intimacy of Sonship, rather than on the basis of servanthood alone.

'You are no more strangers and foreigners, but fellow-citizens with the saints, and of the household of God' (Ephesians 2:19, KJV).

9:18-20 'Therefore even the first covenant was not inaugurated without blood. For when every command had been spoken by Moses to all the people according to the Law, he took the blood of the calves and the goats, with water and scarlet wool and hyssop, and sprinkled both the book itself and all the people, saying "This is the blood of the covenant, which God commanded you."'

Blood paid a central role in the outworking of the first covenant. Leviticus (17:11) states that 'The life of the flesh is in the blood, and I have given it to you on the altar to make atonement for your souls; for it is the blood by reason of the life that makes atonement.' The many animal sacrifices gave the Holy Place the appearance of an abattoir. There was a natural spring on Mount Moriah, on which the Temple was situated, the water from which was used to wash away the copious quantities of blood into the drainage channels constructed around the altar that drained into the Kidron valley. [31] The people and the sacred items were all shown to be cleansed by the sprinkling of the out-poured blood. The Greek can be rendered as stating that the 'book' ('***biblion***' - 'scroll') was sprinkled. It can also be rendered: 'For after every commandment of the law had been recited by Moses to all the people, he took the blood of the calves, and of the goats, with water and scarlet wool, and the book itself, and sprinkled all the people.' [32]

The correct meaning is clearly expressed in the Old Testament passage being referred to. Exodus 24:6-8: 'Moses took half of the blood and put it in basins, and the other half of the blood he sprinkled on the altar. Then he took the book of the covenant and read it in the hearing of the people; and they said, "All that the Lord has spoken we will do, and we will be obedient!" So Moses took the blood and sprinkled it on the people, and said, "Behold the blood of the covenant, which the Lord has made with you in accordance with all these words."' It was the people who were sprinkled, not the book. The idea that Jews would sprinkle blood on their precious Torah scrolls, thus rendering them illegible, is a curiosity that is not found to be based on the actual Jewish practice related in the Old Testament scriptures. The hyssop plant used for the purpose was tied together using scarlet wool and dipped in the basin of blood and then in water this making the sticky blood (prone to clotting) better able to be sprinkled, as may be seen from Leviticus (14:51-52) where it is referred to in relation to the cleaning of the house of a leper. 'He shall take the cedar wood and the hyssop and the scarlet string, with the live bird, and dip them in the blood of the slain bird as well as in the running water, and sprinkle the house seven times. He shall thus cleanse the house with the blood of the bird and with the running water, along with the live bird and with the cedar wood and with the hyssop and with the scarlet string.'

The words, 'This is the blood of the covenant, which God commanded you', resonate with the liturgy of the Seder (Passover meal) service taken by Jesus at his 'last supper'. 'When he had taken a cup and given thanks, he gave it to them, saying, "Drink from it, all of you; for this is my blood of the covenant, which is poured out for many for forgiveness of sins"' (Matthew 26:27-28).

9:21-25 'And in the same way he sprinkled both the tabernacle and all the vessels of the ministry with the blood. And according to the Law, one may almost say all things are cleansed with blood, and without shedding of blood there is no forgiveness. Therefore it was necessary for the copies of the things in the heavens to be cleansed with these, but the heavenly things themselves with better sacrifices than these. For Christ did not enter a holy place made with hands, a mere copy of the true one, but

into heaven itself, now to appear in the presence of God for us; nor was it that he would offer himself often, as the high priest enters the holy place year by year with blood that is not his own.'

The words of the Torah-scrolls were considered to be intrinsically sacred and to be obeyed (Deuteronomy 25:58). There was therefore no need to continually cleanse them with the sprinkled blood. Items made and handled by men ('copies' of the heavenly realities), even though used for sacred purposes, were not in the same category, and were consequently cleansed before use in mediation between God and man. From Genesis 3:21 on (when God slew an animal to make skins with which to clothe Adam and Eve following their sin) God required that the seriousness of sin be recognised by the offering of an animal, the life of which would stand in the place of the life of the sinner. Jesus' final mediatory sacrifice had the once-and-for-all effect of cleansing the stain of human sin and allowing a restoration of the fellowship between God and man, in the power of the Holy Spirit. His blood was the 'better sacrifice' that was poured out in heaven, in an on-going act of atonement for the sin of everyone.

9:26-28 'Otherwise he would have needed to suffer often since the foundation of the world; but now once at the consummation of the ages he has been manifested to put away sin by the sacrifice of himself. And inasmuch as it is appointed for men to die once and after this comes judgment, so Christ also, having been offered once to bear the sins of many will appear a second time for salvation, without reference to sin, to those who eagerly await him.'

Jesus' 'suffering' (the Greek here is *'paschô'* - 'passion') needs never to be repeated. The word for 'world' here is *'**kosmos**'* ('the created order') to which God, the ultimate master-builder, laid the foundation. Jesus' sacrifice is spoken of as being made at the 'consummation' ('*suntcleia*' - 'completion', from '*sunteleô*' - 'to finish') of the age ('*aiôn*' - the Greek is in the singular not the pleural). Jesus' death closed the 'age' of the Law and the offerings for sin that the Tabernacle and Temple represented; there was no further need for them. Within a single generation of Jesus' death the fate of the Temple and all those within the walls of its courts was sealed by the invading Roman army under the command of Vespasian. So too humankind dies but once (there is no re-incarnation), after which God's righteous judgement will occur.

Jesus has already been judged (and found acceptable) on behalf of those who are found 'in Christ' and part of the new covenant household family of God. Believer's works will be judged (1 Corinthians 3:11-15), [xxii] and what is of God, having been initiated by him, will last as fruit into eternity. The remainder (that which is not of faith, and so is sin in God's eyes ('Whatever is not from faith is sin' - Romans 14:23), will be consumed by the purifying fire that the Apostle Paul describes our being saved through.

Those who are in relationship with Christ can eagerly await ('*apekdechomai*' - 'assiduously and patiently wait for') his return when we will see Jesus face to face, and not be greeted with reproach but with delight. All sin will have been washed away and all guilt removed. Our service of him will be graciously assessed and that which is self-glorifying and corrupt will be burned away so that we will never again be burdened by it. But every little act, word, thought

---

[xxii] 1 Corinthians 3:11-15: 'For no man can lay a foundation other than the one which is laid, which is Jesus Christ. Now if any man builds on the foundation with gold, silver, precious stones, wood, hay, straw, each man's work will become evident; for the day will show it because it is to be revealed with fire, and the fire itself will test the quality of each man's work. If any man's work which he has built on it remains, he will receive a reward. If any man's work is burned up, he will suffer loss; but he himself will be saved, yet so as through fire.'

that our Father can find worthy of praise will receive reward. In a final act of salvation we will receive new and eternal bodies that are incorruptible, made of the same stuff as the body of Jesus - bodies of glory. What a moment that will be, something we should indeed be eagerly anticipating.

Chapter 10

Jesus - 'Written about in the Scroll; come to do your will, O God'

10:1-2 'For the Law, since it has only a shadow of the good things to come and not the very form of things, can never, by the same sacrifices which they offer continually year by year, make perfect those who draw near. Otherwise would they not have ceased to be offered, because the worshippers, having once been cleansed, would no longer have had consciousness of sins?'

The Law was a 'shadow' of something occurring afterwards in time and which, in the light emanating from heaven, cast an outlined image that was like the thing that came after but not at all the same thing. The writer is challenging his audience to choose between relating to the shadow or to the reality, and especially in the light of their knowledge of the shadow's inability to help at their point of need - sin. The Law was given in large part to demonstrate the futility of attempting to live up to God's 'righteous requirements' in one's own strength, and so points to the need all mankind has for a Saviour. Galatians 3:24 [xxiii] describes the Law as a tutor or guardian that had a temporary rule until faith in Christ was reached, acting rather like a policeman or jailer (Galatians 3:23) who could point out sin but not remedy the underlying problem that was the cause. Consequently perfection under the Law was never attained, because the 'perfect' (Christ) had not yet come.

[xxiii] Galatians 3:23-24: 'Before faith came, we were kept in custody under the law, being shut up to the faith which was later to be revealed. Therefore the Law has become our tutor to lead us to Christ, so that we may be justified by faith.'

If the Law could in fact have saved there would have been no need for the horrendous experience that Jesus underwent in our place at Calvary. The Law not only revealed to us our shortcomings in relation to God's standards; it also provoked the sinful natures in us by revealing to them what is right and so aggravating the underlying rebellious attitudes that keep us from obeying God. (Romans 7:9 - 'When the commandment came, sin became alive and I died.') The commandment informed us exactly what God's standards were, and then 'sin' in us then took delight in breaking them. While faith in the promises of God was possible (as Abraham had shown), the Law (including the rabbinic Oral Law) dominated their society with its rules and regulations.

'Consciousness' of sin (the Greek is '*suneidêsis*', also meaning 'conscience') prompted those who wanted to please God to seek a way to atone for their wrongdoing by means of sacrifices and offerings. These had to be offered on a regular basis to deal with the continuing problem of sin. Through faith in Jesus' death on the cross, we 'die' to both Law [xxiv] and sin, [xxv] and are raised in baptism to a new spiritual life that works from within. The Holy Spirit embarks on a process of inner reformation that our outward cooperation with (teaching, changing behaviour, prayer etc.) supports but cannot replace. It is the indwelling of the Spirit that is a mark of true faith: 'This is how we know that he lives in us: we know it by the Spirit he gave us' (1 John 3:24, NIV). The old ownership by the slave-master of sin is replaced with a new master, Christ. 'Christ redeemed us

---

[xxiv] Galatians 2:19-21 'Through the Law I died to the Law, so that I might live to God. I have been crucified with Christ; and it is no longer I who live, but Christ lives in me; and the life which I now live in the flesh I live by faith in the Son of God, who loved me and gave himself up for me. I do not nullify the grace of God, for if righteousness comes through the Law, then Christ died needlessly.'

[xxv] Romans 6:2-3 'How shall we who died to sin still live in it? Or do you not know that all of us who have been baptized into Christ Jesus have been baptized into his death?'

from the curse of the Law, having become a curse for us' (Galatians 3:13).

10:3-7 'But in those sacrifices there is a reminder of sins year by year. For it is impossible for the blood of bulls and goats to take away sins. Therefore, when he comes into the world, he says, "Sacrifice and offering you have not desired, but a body you have prepared for me; in whole burnt offerings and *sacrifices for* sin you have taken no pleasure." Then I said, "Behold I have come (in the scroll of the book it is written of me) to do your will, O God."'

The shed blood of bulls and goats provided a graphic reminder of the Israelites on-going problem of sin and the futility of repetitive sacrifice to change their underlying rebellious natures. Though God had commanded them they did not bring about the righteous lives that God desired. The writer quotes Psalm 40:6-8, which reads: 'Sacrifice and meal offering you have not desired; my ears you have opened; burnt offering and sin offering you have not required. Then I said, "Behold I come; in the scroll of the book it is written of me. I delight to do your will, O my God; your law is within my heart."' Animal sacrifices played a large part in the educational purposes of God through generation after generation, day after day, year after year. It would have become increasingly clear to any Israelite who was spiritually alert that no amount of sacrifice for sin involving the death of animals made any change to them. To those whose eyes were open, it would become increasingly clear that something new was required. A small proportion of them perhaps saw in the message of the prophets the coming of the Messiah to fulfil the Law of sacrifices and offerings.

The Greek Old Testament (Septuagint) from which the writer quotes, has the phrase, 'A body you have prepared for me' in place of 'My ears you have opened'. The Psalm is now revealed as not simply the prayer of David but also as prophetically inspired words concerning the Lord Jesus Christ. It is a 'messianic Psalm', one that sets out Jesus' mission from his perspective as a true Son-Servant of his Father. Jesus lived a perfect life. He could say to his most-critical enemies, 'Which of you can convict me of sin?' (John 8:46). 'Sin' is '*hamartia*' meaning 'to miss the mark' in relation to the Jewish law. The question can be paraphrased as: 'In what way can you show that I have broken the Law?' Jesus' perfect life meant that he never needed to offer sacrifice or offering for any sin or personal breach of the Law. Sacrifice and offering for sin were 'not required' of him. In a society which focussed on the importance of the Day of Atonement for dealing annually with personal wrong-doing, there is no evidence of Jesus ever participating in it. It is likely to have been this apparent deviation from the conventional Jewish calendar that contributed to his enemies calling him a Samaritan (John 8:48), because the Samaritans followed a different religious calendar. [33]

God the Father prepared a 'body' of a human embryo implanted in the womb of the virgin Mary for the eternal second person of the Trinity to inhabit. The 'scroll of the book' of Isaiah (7:14) reads: 'The Lord himself will give you a sign; behold, a virgin will be with child and bear a son, and she will call his name Immanuel.' 'Young women' at the time of Isaiah were de facto virgins, and the Greek Septuagint version of the Old Testament renders Isaiah's Hebrew word '*almah*' as '*parthenos*', clarifying the meaning as being a literal virgin and not simply a young woman. The New Testament Greek simply follows this line of thought.

Both Jesus and his mother Mary, like King David in Psalm 40 verse 8, delighted to commit themselves to the will of God. As Mary said, "Behold, the bondslave of the Lord; may it be done to me according to your word" (Luke 1:38). In Christ, we follow Jesus' example of offering himself to God. As Paul wrote to the churches in Rome, 'I urge you, brethren, by the mercies of God, to present your bodies a living and holy sacrifice, acceptable to God, which is your spiritual service of worship. And do not be conformed to this world, but be transformed by the renewing of your mind, so that you may prove what the will of God is, that which is good and acceptable and perfect.' It is this 'renewing of our minds' in conformity with God's word that allows us to take hold of God's intentions for us.

10:8-10 'After saying above, 'Sacrifices and offerings and whole burnt offerings and *sacrifices for* sin you have not desired, nor have you taken pleasure in them' (which are offered according to the Law), then he said, "Behold I have come to do your will." He takes away the first in order to establish the second.'

The writer lists the measures taken for sin that God had established under the Law but in which he took 'no pleasure' because of the backdrop of sin that they stood as remedies for. 'Sacrifices' here is '*thusia*' (the 'victim', as Isaac had briefly been), 'offering' is '*prosphora*' ('the act of giving a gift'), 'whole burnt offering' is '*holokautoma*', from '*holokautos*', (the 'burning' that the animals were subject to, and from which the word 'holocaust' is derived), and finally '*hamartia*'. The last is the common New Testament word for sin ('to miss the mark'), so how is it that it becomes listed with the three other words for sin-offerings?

The answer is that the main Hebrew words for 'sin' and 'sin-offering' were one and the same ('*asham*' and '*chattath*'). This can lead to confusion, and it is the context that determines which use is meant. The Jewish writer of Hebrews is using the word '*hamartia*' in the conventional Jewish way, which includes the meaning of 'sin-offering', even though this has a very different meaning to 'sin'.

It must always be borne in mind that the men God used to pen the New Testament were for the most part Jews, writing very often to

Jews about a Jew (Jesus). They had to convert their Hebrew thought into the lingua franca of their day (Greek). The word 'sacrifices' appears in italics in verses 6 and 8 because it is not in the Greek text. The passage clearly is not intended to read 'and sin you have not desired' - there has never been any evidence that God ever 'desired sin'! Jesus offered perfect obedience to his Father, all the way to the cross, as a sin-offering (the alternative meaning of '*hamartia*'. The coming of the perfect 'second' (Jesus), means that God has no longer any need for the first and imperfect animal model of dealing with sin and its consequences.

10:10-14 'By this will we have been sanctified through the offering of the body of Jesus Christ once for all. Every priest stands daily, ministering and offering time after time the same sacrifices, which can never take away sins; but he, having offered one sacrifice for sins for all time, sat down at the right hand of God, waiting from that time onward until his enemies be made a footstool for his feet. For by one offering he has perfected for all time those who are sanctified.'

'By this will' is '*thelema*', meaning 'According to his pleasure and desire'. We have been 'made holy ('*hagiazo*' - 'sanctified') through this offering of the person of the Lord Jesus Christ himself. As Peter wrote, 'His divine power has granted to us everything pertaining to life and godliness, through the true knowledge of him who called us by his own glory and excellence. For by these he has granted to us his precious and magnificent promises, so that by them you may become partakers of the divine nature.' The 'knowledge' that Peter speaks of here is '*epignôsis*', which denotes the full and personalized knowledge born of one's own experience. As we take hold of the promises that God has spoken to us in his word we are changed by the power of that word into his likeness.

The futility of the priest's daily sacrifices is again exposed and compared with the finality of Jesus' own sacrifice, which returned him to his rightful place at the Father's right hand, accompanied by the praise and glory that his sacrifice warranted. Jesus' superiority over the priests is further illustrated by his seated posture in comparison with the priests who stood to minister. At the end of the present age all creation will be brought to a close, including his enemies, who will take their rightful place - under his feet. As David had prophesied in Psalm 110:1, 'The Lord says to my Lord, "Sit at my right hand, until I make your enemies a footstool for your feet."' And as Paul confirmed, 'He must reign until he has put all his enemies under his feet' (1 Corinthians 15:25). Jesus' sacrifice, as has been previously said, was once-and-for-all. The 'perfection' that it brings is '*teleioo*', meaning 'complete'. Nothing else needs to be added to us other than Christ's offering, it is fully sufficient for '*hagiazo*' - being 'made holy'.

The outworking of this amazing truth is that in the strictest possible sense we cannot now say that we are sinners in the sense of our primary identity. We are 'sinners saved by grace' - people who were sinners but who have now been saved by grace out of the state of sin as a result of God's unmerited favour. We are now the '*hagiazo*', or as that is often translated into English, 'saints' - not in the 'stained-glass' window sense, but in the down-to-earth and practical way that the Lord Jesus Christ modelled for us to follow. An essential change in our nature has taken place through our trust in what Jesus has done. This does not mean we are perfect. But it means that when we sin we are reverting to the lifestyle of an identity that is no longer ours. We are 'saints' of God. A permanent total change has taken place in our nature and our identity and also in our destiny, not just in this life, but for eternity.

10:15-18 'And the Holy Spirit also testifies to us; for after saying, "This is the covenant that I will make with them

after those days", says the Lord. "I will put my laws upon their heart, and on their mind I will write them." He then says, "Their sins and their lawless deeds I will remember no more."' Now where there is forgiveness of these things, there is no longer any offering for sin.'

The writer reminds them again of the word spoken by God the Holy Spirit through the prophet Jeremiah. "'Behold, days are coming," declares the Lord when I will make a new covenant with the house of Israel and with the house of Judah, not like the covenant which I made with their fathers in the day I took them by the hand to bring them out of the land of Egypt, my covenant which they broke, although I was a husband to them," declares the Lord. "But this is the covenant which I will make with the house of Israel after those days," declares the Lord, "I will put my law within them and on their heart I will write it; and I will be their God, and they shall be my people. They will not teach again each man his neighbour and each man his brother, saying, "Know the Lord," for they will all know me, from the least of them to the greatest of them," declares the Lord, "for I will forgive their iniquity, and their sin I will remember no more"' (Jeremiah 31:31-34).

The new covenant was to involve not the Law being taken on 'tablets' of stone, but rather an 'intra-cardiac' administration by the indwelling of the Holy Spirit. The Spirit would impress God's Law and intentions upon the heart, and so bring about a spiritual change from within that would bring a new spiritual birth. The law of the Spirit of life sets us free from the law of sin and death (Romans 8:2). The new covenant involved the Son of God's own blood being shed for sin, a much more complete and efficacious sacrifice that leaves any further offering redundant. The cleansing that has been won for us by Jesus is total and permanent. The outcome of this place of grace is that our confession of sin brings instant restoration and opens again the floodgates of heaven so the Holy Spirit pours into us.

The same Holy Spirit that was given to him without limit, being one with him in person and nature, is similarly given to us 'without measure'. [xxvi]

10:19-22 'Therefore, brethren, since we have confidence to enter the holy place by the blood of Jesus, by a new and living way which he inaugurated for us through the veil, that is, his flesh, and since we have a great priest over the house of God, let us draw near with a sincere heart in full assurance of faith, having our hearts sprinkled clean from an evil conscience and our bodies washed with pure water.'

The idea of entering the Holy of Holies ('*hagios*') described here is the same term as used in chapter 9 verse 3 to signify the innermost part of the tabernacle. This was off-limits to all Jews save the High Priest, and him only once a year; the idea of unlimited access for all would have been and still is a very extraordinary one. Anyone else entering could expect to be struck dead. 'Confidence' here is '*parrêsia*' - 'boldness', necessary given the fearsome consequences that such an approach would have met with under the Old Covenant. The blood of Jesus opens the previously prohibited way into God's presence to all who believe. The veil is the innermost curtain, which the Mishnah records as being 'a hand-breadth' thick. [34] It was 'torn in two from top to bottom' (Matthew 27:51) at the point of Jesus death on the cross, a tearing that the writer presents as a typological figure of Jesus' own body, pierced on the cross as part of his sacrifice.

'Sincere' here is '*alêthinos*', meaning 'true' or 'truthful'. Faith is the confident expectation of God's leading that prompts us to respond to his word to us, a word that itself has the power to engender this

---

[xxvi] John 3:34 'He gives the Spirit without measure.'

disposition of active trust within us. The 'assurance' that this faith is linked with is itself another form of God-given confidence ('***plerophoria***' - 'certain confidence'), a concept closely linked to the 'hope' of verse 23.

The power of Jesus' shed blood transforms the hearts of those who receive him and his word into their lives. Their consciences are re-aligned with spiritual truth, and this new-birth enables a fresh beginning in God's grace and most merciful love. 'Washing' may represent both baptism and the daily washing with the word of God, which Paul speaks of in Ephesians (5:26): 'Cleansed... by the washing of water with the word.' God washes away sin's stains, because 'where sin abounded, grace abounded much more'. The Greek here is '***huperperisseuô***'. '***Perisseuo***' means 'abounded', and '***huper***' is the word from which the English word 'hyper' ('more than') is derived. Where sin abounded, grace 'hyper' abounded. Sin, if brought into the torrent of the grace of God, cannot stand, but is washed away in a flood that is more efficacious than any waterfall.

10:23-25 'Let us hold fast the confession of our hope without wavering, for he who promised is faithful; and let us consider how to stimulate one another to love and good deeds, not forsaking our own assembling together, as is the habit of some, but encouraging one another; and all the more as you see the day drawing near.'

'Hope' ('***elpis***') also means a sense of 'confident expectation' based on faith, very different from the 'fingers-crossed' modern understanding of the word. Hope exists in relationship to 'faith' ('***pistis***'), which itself expresses the active response of trust to God's word spoken to us - 'hope' is the sure confidence that what God has spoken will come to pass. 'Confession' is, again, '***homologeô***' - to 'speak out the same thing in agreement'. 'Agreeing' with what God says is key, as Eliphaz counselled Job: 'Agree with God, and be at peace; in this way good will come to you. Receive instruction from his mouth, and lay up his words in your heart' (Job 22:21-22, NRSV). The consequences are good too - 'You will pray to him, and he will hear you; and you will pay your vows. You will also decree a thing, and it will be established for you; and light will shine on your ways' (Job 22:27-28). Hearing from God (either in his written word or by the '*rhema*' word his Spirit brings) and 'saying the same thing' in agreement with it is integral to rendering our faith effective.

The fruit of this faith is intended to be obvious, not least in the outworking of community (love, good deeds and assembling together) it brings. Jewish converts to Messiah had the loss of strong societal ties to consider before the new community of the church was fully established. The status of apostate and loss of the strong relational support network for the Jewish men and women who embraced the new covenant faith was a major hurdle to overcome. Wavering would be a problem for the majority of converts; their grasp of the fact that a faithful God had a grasp of them was key to continuing their walk with him. Mutual love among the new covenant community was to be 'stimulated' - '*paroxusmos*' - 'provoked' or 'incited' in a positive manner. Their lives were lived with an expectation of the immanency of Christ's return ('You come behind in no gift; waiting for the coming of our Lord Jesus Christ' - 1 Corinthians 1:7, KJV); their assemblies were to be occasions for mutual strengthening and encouragement.

10:26-29 'For if we go on sinning wilfully after receiving the knowledge of the truth, there no longer remains a sacrifice for sins, but a terrifying expectation of judgment and the fury of a fire which will consume the adversaries. Anyone who has set aside the Law of Moses dies without mercy on the testimony of two or three witnesses. How much severer punishment do you think he will deserve who has trampled underfoot the Son of God,

and has regarded as unclean the blood of the covenant by which he was sanctified, and has insulted the Spirit of grace?'

Continuing to deliberately sin may be a sign that the new birth has not actually happened, or it may indicate an exercise of the freewill to turn away from God. 'Knowledge' is, again, '*epignôsis*', meaning a personally acquired full knowledge of something. The writer makes the point that there is no alternative way to atone for sin, no 'Plan B'. There is only the prospect of an eternity separated from the Creator's love. The God who destroyed Sodom and Gomorrah is still very much alive and well, and one day the current age of grace and peace that Jesus' birth and death introduced will end with his return as Judge.

The Law of Moses could not be set aside without consequences, and those who reject Jesus' rescue-mission performed on their behalf have only their own righteousness to fall back on, righteousness that the prophet Isaiah likened to legally unclean menstrual towels. Regarding Jesus' blood as unclean is to treat it like women's menstrual loss, a severe insult indeed in that society. 'Trampled' here is '*katapateô*' - to tread upon and insult, like swine on pearls (Matthew 7:6), an insult that extends from God's Son to his Holy Spirit. God does not withdraw from believers the freewill that they engaged in coming to him in the first place, and while such apostasy is rare it was certainly something that deeply concerned the writer to the Hebrews. Apostasy is not something that the believer can unwittingly fall into. It is the deliberate, thought-out rejection and trampling underfoot of the Son of God, not an inadvertent rejection or a sudden loss of temper.. It is also a despising of the blood of the covenant that made holy, regarding it as something offensive. It is to very deliberately insult the Spirit of grace, in other words, a process of rejection which is coldly thought through and determined in advance. It is simply not possible to do this by accident.

10:30-31 'For we know him who said, "Vengeance is mine, I will repay." And again, "The Lord will judge his people." It is a terrifying thing to fall into the hands of the living God.'

Old Covenant believers most certainly knew God as a God of vengeance and retribution (Deuteronomy 32:35-36).[xxvii] As Moses had said, 'For the Lord your God is a consuming fire, a jealous God.' Many modern believers have lost sight of the fact that God's nature has not and cannot change. The grace and mercy shown in Christ completes the revealing of his character but does not alter the fact of God's justice, justice that requires sinners to repent or take the consequences. Jesus himself will separate the sheep from the goats (Matthew 25:33). For those who know him, his Father's hands are hands of love. For those who reject him there is only the 'fury of fire' that Isaiah had foretold. Isaiah 29:6 - 'From the Lord of hosts you will be punished with thunder and earthquake and loud noise, with whirlwind and tempest and the flame of a consuming fire.' There is only one other allegiance for someone who has rejected Christ and turned away from the grace of God. By doing so, they have aligned themselves with the devil and all the legions of hell. In such a situation, they have no other destination than which Jesus described (Matthew 25:41) as 'the eternal fire prepared for the devil and his angels'. People who align themselves with Satan come under the same judgement as he does. There is no middle ground.

10:32-35 'Remember those earlier days after you had received the light, when you stood your ground in a great contest in the face of suffering. Sometimes you were publicly exposed to insult and persecution; at other times you stood side by side with those who were so treated.

[xxvii] 'It is mine to avenge; I will repay... The Lord will judge his people and have compassion on his servants' (Deuteronomy 32:35-36, NIV)

You sympathized with those in prison and joyfully accepted the confiscation of your property, because you knew that you yourselves had better and lasting possessions. So do not throw away your confidence; it will be richly rewarded.'

'Standing side by side' with persecuted brothers and sisters is something that eastern Christians and others in situations of persecution find strangely lacking from their more secure Western brethren. Organisations like the Barnabas Fund [35] are to be highly commended for their work helping to redress this balance. The 'contest' referred to is '***athlesis***' from '***athleo***', 'to engage in the public (athletic) games'. These games are watched by the crowd of witnesses that the writer will shortly go on to describe in chapter 11. 'Suffering' here is '***pathema***', the term Paul uses to encapsulate Christ's sufferings (his 'passion'), something that he advised the Philippians he was called to share in. [xxviii] And to the Corinthians: 'Just as the sufferings of Christ are ours, so also our comfort is abundant through Christ' (2 Corinthians 1:5).

A 'sharing' in Jesus' suffering is part of Christian maturation, something Paul made no bones about. 'I rejoice in my sufferings for you, and fill up that which is behind of the afflictions of Christ in my flesh for his body's sake, which is the church' (Colossians 1:24, KJV). The Hebrew believer's experience is very similar to that undergone by the persecuted church in China, Islamic states and the former Soviet Union. When met with faith and trust in the God who watches over us, these sufferings and trials serve to store up an eternal reward in heaven, where Jesus said, "Where neither moth nor

---

[xxviii] Philippians 3:10-11: 'That I may know him and the power of his resurrection and the fellowship of his sufferings, being conformed to his death; in order that I may attain to the resurrection from the dead.'

rust destroys, and where thieves do not break in or steal" (Matthew 6:20). These 'possessions' are truly ever-lasting. It is the testimony of the whole New Testament that suffering and glory are inextricably entwined. There is no expectation of one without the other. If we long to share the glory of the Lord Jesus - and we should - we will inevitably share the sufferings.

10:36-39 'For you have need of endurance, so that when you have done the will of God, you may receive what was promised. 'For yet in a very little while, he who is coming will come, and will not delay. But my righteous one shall live by faith; but if he shrinks back, my soul has no pleasure in him.' But we are not of those who shrink back to destruction, but of those who have faith to the preserving of the soul.'

'Endurance' here is '*hupomonê*' ('steadfast patience') from '*menô*' ('to abide'). God's will is something that the attitude of faith allows us to relax into, just as sitting down on a chair allows us to transfer all our weight off ourselves and onto the chair. Then we can, without striving to grasp, receive things that God has promised to freely give us. The imminence of Jesus' return is again emphasised, a meeting that could take place at any moment for any one; no one knows with certainty the hour of his return (Matthew 24:36) or the hour of one's own death. Either bring about the end of this life and the entry into the full salvation of an eternal immortal body. The writer quotes from the prophet Habakkuk (2:3), who similarly encouraged God's people to hold fast to what they had received from God. 'Shrink back' (*hupostolê*' - 'the timidity of one stealthily retreating') [36] expresses the timidity of an orphan, not the confident trust of a son or daughter. 'Living by faith' means an attitude of complete dependency on a heavenly Father who works through us rather than our working for him in our own strengths. Depending on God-given strengths and abilities rather than on the God who gave them is a recipe for frustration and weariness.

'Preserving' the soul is '*peripoiêsis*', meaning to enter into one's inheritance and to the final possession of us ourselves by Almighty God. As Paul wrote to the church at Ephesus, 'You were sealed in him with the Holy Spirit of promise, who is given as a pledge of our inheritance, with a view to the redemption of God's own possession, to the praise of his glory' (Ephesians 1:13-14). As Paul said twice in writing to the Thessalonians, 'God has not destined us for wrath, but for obtaining salvation through our Lord Jesus Christ' (1 Thessalonians 5:9), and, 'He called you by our gospel, to the obtaining of the glory of our Lord Jesus Christ' (2 Thessalonians 2:14, KJV). The alternative to receiving this 'gracious gift of life' (1 Peter 3:7) from God is 'destruction' ('*apoleia*' from '*olethros*'- 'destruction').

Chapter 11

Jesus - perfecting the saints' faith

11:1-2 'Now faith is the assurance of things hoped for, the conviction of things not seen. For by it the men of old gained approval.'

Faith is sometimes popularly described as 'blind'; the truth is the exact opposite. It has sufficient visual acuity to be able to see the invisible, within the spiritual realm where the God who ordains everything dwells. 'Hope' is '***elpizo***', the calm 'confidence' that the assurance of faith brings, and which enables us to take hold of God's promises. 'Conviction' is '***elegchos***', meaning 'evidence' and consequential 'conviction' of truth; our faith is based 'convincing proofs' (Acts 1:3). [xxix] The Christian faith is based upon historic facts; Jesus' historicity and death has been established many times over from Roman and Jewish extra-biblical sources. The empty tomb following the posting of a Roman guard to watch over Pilate's seal evidences Jesus' resurrection. Unable to produce a dead body and end all speculation, the authorities could only resort to threatening those converted by Jesus' many bodily appearances and the witness of those whose lives he changed.

The 'approval' gained by those who found faith is '***martureô***', meaning their 'testimony' or 'witness', which for many of the characters described was a witness unto death. Overcoming in the faith gains God's approval and his reward of an 'imperishable crown', unlike the Greek games which offered a perishable, though

---

[xxix] Acts 1:3 'He also presented himself alive after his suffering, by many convincing proofs, appearing to them over a period of forty days and speaking of the things concerning the kingdom of God.'

highly valued wreath of olive leaves. 'Everyone who competes for the prize is temperate in all things. Now they do it to obtain a perishable crown, but we for an imperishable crown' (1 Corinthians 9:25, NKJV). Athletes go to extreme lengths to gain Olympic medals; in the writer's day the same attitude was in evidence in their competitions. The Christian life offers much more substantial rewards that will last in and through eternity.

11:3 'By faith we understand that the worlds were prepared by the word of God, so that what is seen was not made out of things which are visible.'

Genesis chapter 1 reveals the creative power of God's spoken word, a word God has not ceased to speak. As Psalm 50:1-3 states, 'The Mighty One, God the Lord, speaks and summons the earth, from the rising of the sun to the place where it sets. From Zion, perfect in beauty, God shines forth. Our God comes and will not be silent.' God's spoken word created the invisible atoms and electronic particles responsible for holding matter together, as well as the 'ages' ('*aiôn*' - 'worlds') - the successive periods of time that his creation exists within. 'Prepared' here is '*katartizô*', meaning to 'render fit for' or 'repair'. God's word has an on-going role, when declared in faith by his people, to keep the ages in which we live in a right state of repair. In this way we are the preservative salt that Jesus spoke of. "You are the salt of the earth; but if the salt loses its flavour, how shall it be seasoned? It is then good for nothing but to be thrown out and trampled underfoot by men" (Matthew 5:13).

11:4 'By faith Abel offered to God a better sacrifice than Cain, through which he obtained the testimony that he was righteous, God testifying about his gifts, and through faith, though he is dead, he still speaks.'

Abel's sacrifice was 'better' ('*polus*' - 'greater' in terms of quality), being born of faith. He also followed the example and word of God regarding the 'righteous' ('right towards God') animal sacrifice that God himself had made in clothing the fallen Adam and Eve after their sin in the Garden of Eden. Cain's rebellious heart was made plain by the 'doing my own thing' sacrifice of the produce that the work of his own hands had brought him. It was further and even more grossly manifest in the murder of his brother Abel. Abel 'still spoke' after his death; his shed blood cried out (figuratively) to God from the ground and God heard (Genesis 4:10), because God had witnessed the murder occur. Abel's 'right relationship' with God gave him access to God both in life and in death.

11:5-6 'By faith Enoch was taken up so that he would not see death; and he was not found because God took him up; for he obtained the witness that before his being taken up he was pleasing to God. And without faith it is impossible to please him, for he who comes to God must believe that he is and that he is a rewarder of those who seek him.'

Enoch was a man of such close relationship with God that he did not experience death in the conventional manner. Genesis 5:22-24 relates: 'Then Enoch walked with God three hundred years after he became the father of Methuselah, and he had other sons and daughters. So all the days of Enoch were three hundred and sixty-five years. Enoch walked with God; and he was not, for God took him.' This was a product of a relationship that Enoch had evidently actively chosen for, and a similar choice is open to all. Of Jesus' twelve disciples three (Peter, James and John) were especially close to him, but John was closest of all, leaning on Christ at his last Seder (Passover) meal (John 13:23 and 21:20) and remaining at the cross after the other men had fled (John 19:26). Although John was Jesus' cousin (John's mother Salome and Mary were sisters), John still had to make a choice to stay close to him, and many years earlier Enoch had made a similar choice.

This level of intimacy is always a choice that is pleasing to the God who made man expressly for the purpose of being in close relationship with him. We please God when we demonstrate an attitude of absolute reliance upon him rather than on the gifts and abilities he has graciously bestowed on us. When we lean on God ('believe' is '***pisteou***' meaning an active trust, similar to the trust exhibited when sitting down and transferring our weight onto a chair) rather than relying on ourselves, we please him and can experience him working more powerfully through us. He then guides us into works he has prepared in advance for us to do, thereby producing fruit that will remain for an eternal reward. As Jesus said, 'I chose you, and appointed you that you would go and bear fruit, and that your fruit would remain' (John 15:16). Only this attitude of faith towards God can produce fruit that pleases him. All other works smell to him of human reliance, the 'filthy rags' (Isaiah 64:6) of our own efforts done on his behalf, but not in fact born of him.

All believers will similarly be taken up to meet their Lord, be it from death or from life. 'The Lord himself will descend from heaven with a shout, with the voice of the archangel and with the trumpet of God, and the dead in Christ will rise first. Then we who are alive and remain will be caught up together with them in the clouds to meet the Lord in the air' (1 Thessalonians 4:17). For this reason, together with our not knowing exactly when this might occur, or indeed when we will die, we should 'be diligent to be found by him in peace, spotless and blameless' (2 Peter 3:14). Once again faith ('believe that he is') is emphasized; it brings eternal rewards. God is referred to as '***misthapodotês***', which means 'One who pays wages', echoing Jesus' teaching regarding the importance of 'storing up treasure in heaven', where it cannot be lost or stolen, but will last for eternity bringing glory to him who 'rewards openly' (Matthew 6:18-21).

11:7 'By faith Noah, being warned by God about things not yet seen, in reverence prepared an ark for the salvation of his household, by which he condemned the world, and became an heir of the righteousness which is according to faith.'

Genesis 6:8 records of Noah that he found '*chen*' ('grace and favour') in God's eyes, something that was the result of his faith (in being pleasing to God). Genesis 6:9 relates that 'Noah was a righteous man (Hebrew: '*tsaddiq*' - 'just', 'right with God' - yet before the Law was given), and blameless (Hebrew: '*tamim*' - 'complete', 'perfect') in his time; Noah walked with God', in other words, just as Enoch had done. His 'right relationship' resulted in him, though a sinner, being regarded by God as 'blameless'. This is only possible by faith, and is exactly what happens to followers of Christ. They enter a 'right relationship' with God by faith in Christ and his sacrifice, and are consequently seen by God as 'blameless'. The Hebrew word '*tamim*' also means 'without spot or blemish', which is exactly as Paul describes how God sees us in Christ - 'The church in all her glory, having no spot or wrinkle or any such thing; but that she would be holy and blameless' (Ephesians 5:27).

Noah pleased God by his attitude of obedient dependency, being willing to build a ship and enter it long before any visible signs of the rain that God had foretold. He had heard from God, believed, and so was 'certain of what he could not see' with his natural eyes - the flood that his spiritual eyes could see. This act of faith stood as a sign of God's judgement to all his neighbours who had been 'eating and drinking, marrying and giving in marriage, until the day that Noah entered into the ark' (Matthew 24:38). They had been carrying on their normal day-to-day lives in complete disregard to God. Noah, on the other hand, had been walking out a living relationship of trust in and obedience to God. Consequently he was a forerunner of all those who would, through trust in Christ, inherit the reward of faith - eternal life.

11:8-10 'By faith Abraham, when he was called, obeyed by going out to a place which he was to receive for an inheritance; and he went out, not knowing where he was going. By faith he lived as an alien in the land of promise, as in a foreign land, dwelling in tents with Isaac and Jacob, fellow heirs of the same promise; for he was looking for the city which has foundations, whose architect and builder is God.'

Continuing his chronological journey through Israel's history, the writer visits that stalwart of faith, Abraham. Abraham, their patriarch, the man who left his home in Ur of the Chaldees to journey with God to a land of promise. Abraham, the man of faith who placed his wife Sara in jeopardy by telling Pharaoh (Genesis 12) that she was his sister. Abraham, the man of faith who, at the time of God repeating that particular test of faith, told Abimelech, King of Gerar (Genesis 20), that, yes indeed, Sara was his sister. Abraham's famous faith was based on his believing God's promise that he would be a father of many nations, but like us all, his trust sometimes faltered. He tried to short-cut God's provision by sleeping with his wife's maid Hagar (Genesis 16). Israel has been in conflict with Hagar's son Ishmael's descendants ever since.

But for all his failings, Abraham heard God's word to him, believed it, and expressed his trust in it by active obedience to it. As such he fulfilled the words of Jesus - 'Everyone who hears these words of mine and acts on them, may be compared to a wise man who built his house on the rock' (Matthew 7:24). He lived, like Moses would later, as 'a stranger in a strange land' (Exodus 2:22). 'Alien' people in foreign countries were often despised and had less rights and recourses than those native-born, but Abraham managed to keep his gaze God-ward, beyond his life on earth and towards heaven far beyond.

Hebrews 11:10 ('Whose architect and builder is God') carries an echo of Proverbs 8:30-31. 'Then I was beside him, as a master workman; and I was daily his delight, rejoicing always, before him, rejoicing in the world, his earth, and having my delight in the sons of men.' 'Workman' is '*amon*', meaning 'architect'. God the Father and Jesus the Son are depicted as an architect and his son working together, just as Joseph, the 'master **tekton**' (Greek: '**architekton**', as used by the Apostle Paul in 1 Corinthians 3:10), would have worked alongside the boy Jesus. Abraham's journey had a nomadic quality to it ('tents'), one that demonstrated the pilgrim nature of his calling. His real home was in the heavenly city that his life was directed towards.

11:11-12 'By faith even Sarah herself received ability to conceive, even beyond the proper time of life, since she considered him faithful who had promised. Therefore there was born even of one man, and him as good as dead at that, as many descendants as the stars of heaven in number, and innumerable as the sand which is by the seashore.'

The real hero of faith in this part of Israel's story is in fact a heroine. Sarah, after her initial mirth (Genesis 18:12, [xxx] as Abraham had also laughed at God's promise - Genesis 17:17) [xxxi], trusts to the point of conception, even willing to trust being passed off twice, without

---

[xxx] Genesis 18:12: 'Sarah laughed to herself, saying, "After I have become old, shall I have pleasure, my lord being old also?"'

[xxxi] Genesis 17:1: 'Then Abraham fell on his face and laughed, and said in his heart, "Will a child be born to a man one hundred years old? And will Sarah, who is ninety years old, bear a child?"'

complaint, as her husband's sister. From Isaac came the many promised descendants, both natural and spiritual. They are innumerable to men; God however knows their number.

11:13-14 'All these died in faith, without receiving the promises, but having seen them and having welcomed them from a distance, and having confessed that they were strangers and exiles on the earth. For those who say such things make it clear that they are seeking a country of their own.'

The promises to the great men and women of faith included the promise of the Messiah. They saw the coming Messiah by faith and welcomed what they saw. They lived as 'strangers' ('*xenos*' - 'foreigners'); resident aliens on earth, citizens of a different kingdom altogether - a heavenly one. 'Confessed' here is, again, '*homologeô*' - 'to say the same thing in agreement'. This 'agreement' with God was what gave them the faith they needed to be able to be detached from their possessions and even their own lives.

11:15-16 'And indeed if they had been thinking of that country from which they went out, they would have had opportunity to return. But as it is, they desire a better country, that is, a heavenly one. Therefore God is not ashamed to be called their God; for he has prepared a city for them.'

God the Father does not force his children to do his will. If one wants something else that is not of itself sinful then God's permitted will usually accommodates that (gives an 'opportunity to return'). He will change the desires of human hearts that are open to him to his own will in his own time. Then we will know the will of God as Paul sets it out to be - 'perfect and pleasing' to us as well as to him. 'You will be able to test and approve what God's will is - his good, pleasing and perfect will' (Romans 12:2, NIV). As Jesus said, there is a place prepared for all of the Father's children. John 14:2: 'In my Father's house are many dwelling places; if it were not so, I would have told you; for I go to prepare a place for you.'

11:17-19 'By faith Abraham, when he was tested, offered up Isaac, and he who had received the promises was offering up his only begotten son; it was he to whom it was said, "In Isaac your descendants shall be called." He considered that God is able to raise people even from the dead, from which he also received him back as a type.'

Abraham approached Mount Moriah, the place of his intended sacrifice of Isaac, with the attitude that 'God will provide for himself the lamb for the burnt offering' (Genesis 22:8). And so it proved, both in the ram caught by its horns in the thicket and in the perfect Son from heaven sacrificed at Calvary many years later. Abraham offered Isaac on the altar believing (because of the promise of Genesis 21:12) [xxxii] that God was able to bring him back to life again, just as Jesus offered himself in trust in the same power of his Father. Isaac too demonstrates a great level of faith and trust in his human father Abraham, who must surely, as God had instructed,[xxxiii] have taught Isaac that necessary spiritual disposition and trust in his heavenly Father as well. 'Type' here is '*parabole*'; a 'parable', as in the many stories Jesus told, meaning 'to cast side by side for the sake

---

[xxxii] Genesis 21:12 'God said to Abraham, "Do not be distressed because of the lad and your maid; whatever, Sarah tells you, listen to her, for through Isaac your descendants shall be named."

[xxxiii] Genesis 18:19 'I have chosen him, so that he may command his children and his household after him to keep the way of the Lord by doing righteousness and justice, so that the Lord may bring upon Abraham what he has spoken about him.'

of comparison'. Abraham receiving Isaac back from (metaphorical) death was a figure of God the Father receiving his Son Jesus back from the place of the dead.

11:20 'By faith Isaac blessed Jacob and Esau, even regarding things to come.'

Isaac trusted in God, being (in all probability) aware of Jacob and Rebekah's deception. 'Jacob came close to Isaac his father, and he felt him and said, "The voice is the voice of Jacob, but the hands are the hands of Esau"... And he said, "Are you really my son Esau?"' (Genesis 27:22 and 24). Isaac was willing to trust, whichever son it was, that God's hand was in the situation, and so is unwilling to revoke it when Esau's later arrival exposes the deception. Esau, having despised his birthright in selling it for a simple meal (Genesis 25:32), was unable despite his protestations to gain anything other than a considerably lesser blessing. Both boys would have heard of God's promises from Abraham himself (who did not die until they were 15 years of age) - "Through us, my boys, all nations on earth will be blessed." Perhaps Esau, having heard it many times, rolled his eyes and longed to go out hunting. But Jacob heard the story with a deeper hunger for God in his heart each time, a hunger known by God, for the significance that only God can give. He longed for his birthright; perhaps Esau was bored by it.

11:21 'By faith Jacob, as he was dying, blessed each of the sons of Joseph, and worshipped, leaning on the top of his staff.'

Faith involves taking hold of the promises of God and acting upon them. Jacob reversed the blessing's traditional age-based order of Ephraim and Manasseh (Genesis 48:14), knowing that God's purposes are sometimes so established, and speaking under the directions of the Holy Spirit. His obedience to God's prophetic direction to the 12 tribal patriarchs was in itself an act of worship. The writer uses the normal Greek word for worship, '*proskuneô*', meaning 'to kiss towards'. '*Kuneô*' is itself from '*kuon*' for dog, the term is descriptive of a pet dog greeting its master with affectionate licking of the hand. Jacob's last act in the weakness preceding death was personal worship given gladly in deep affection to the covenant-keeping God who had never failed him.

11:22 'By faith Joseph, when he was dying, made mention of the exodus of the sons of Israel, and gave orders concerning his bones.'

The writer refers to Genesis 50:24-25. 'Joseph said to his brothers, "I am about to die, but God will surely take care of you and bring you up from this land to the land which he promised on oath to Abraham, to Isaac and to Jacob." Then Joseph made the sons of Israel swear, saying, "God will surely take care of you, and you shall carry my bones up from here." Joseph is fully expectant that God's promises to his forefather's will be fulfilled, and that the people will be led to the Promised Land. His trust is therefore demonstrated in giving his sons his instructions concerning the movement of his body ('bones') so that they stayed within the covenant family of God, rather than be separated from them after death.

11:23 'By faith Moses, when he was born, was hidden for three months by his parents, because they saw he was a beautiful child; and they were not afraid of the king's edict.'

Moses is described as '*asteios*', meaning 'pleasant featured' or 'comely'. That is what made him, with the added appeal of his tears, an attractive child for Pharaoh's daughter to adopt. His parent's were determined to save him from Pharaoh's murderous pronouncement regarding the casting of male Hebrew children to the Nile crocodiles.

This was firstly because they trusted in God's care for them in general and also because they believed that such a child was gifted by God for a set purpose that he would perform.

Moses had said that Messiah would be 'like him', meaning in personhood as well as in mission. 'The Lord your God will raise up for you a prophet like me from among you, from your countrymen' (Deuteronomy 18:15). Moses was a highly educated person, hidden in Pharaoh's palace until his redemptive mission began. Similarly Jesus was hidden in the place of rabbinic wisdom (Bet Midrash, in the Court of Israel), [37] until age 30, the point at which the Oral Law allowed public rabbinic ministry to commence. [38] This is why Stephen refers to Moses' education in his speech to the Sanhedrin (Acts 7:22). [xxxiv] The Sanhedrin were well aware of Jesus' scholastic standing in their society, having overseen his ordination as the brightest Jewish scholar ever to grace the Temple courts.

11:24-26 'By faith Moses, when he had grown-up, refused to be called the son of Pharaoh's daughter, choosing rather to endure ill-treatment with the people of God than to enjoy the passing pleasures of sin, considering the reproach of Christ greater riches than the treasures of Egypt; for he was looking to the reward.'

Moses chose to side with the fate of his own people rather than continue in a privileged and educated position in Pharaoh's palace. In choosing for them rather than for the Egyptians he was sharing in their fate, including the coming of their Messiah, whom he later would say would be a 'Prophet like him' (Deuteronomy 18:15). To share in the people's inheritance in Messiah was worth much more than everything Egypt could ever offer, something just as true today.

[xxxiv] Acts 7:22: 'Moses was educated in all the learning of the Egyptians, and he was a man of power in words and deeds.'

11:27 'By faith he left Egypt, not fearing the wrath of the king; for he endured, as seeing him who is unseen.'

Moses, having killed the Egyptian slave-driver (and so committed manslaughter) had fled Egypt in fear in the direction of Midian (on the eastern coast of the Red Sea). But God led and guided him, and his father-in-law Jethro was also a valuable source of future wisdom (Exodus 18:17-23). Faith can see the invisible; Moses rejected the all-too-visible gods of the Egyptians in favour of the God who was seen by faith, and left Egypt (on the second occasion, after the death of the first-born) convinced that God would make the mission he had been entrusted with succeed. Thus he was able to 'endure' the moaning and complaining of the people that God had placed in his charge.

11:28 'By faith he kept the Passover and the sprinkling of the blood, so that he who destroyed the firstborn would not touch them.'

God's precise instructions in avoiding the death of the firstborn were obeyed to the letter. Moses inaugurated the Passover Festival and so 'kept' it; the Greek here is in the perfect tense, signifying an action which is viewed as having been completed, once and for all, and not needing to be repeated. The lamb's blood did not need to be continually applied to the house's lintels to prevent the destroying anger from entering. Once was sufficient. The annual festival established to celebrate the event both looked back at it and also forwards to the ultimate deliverance from spiritual slavery that Messiah's sacrifice would bring. Moses and the people were saved from the death of their firstborn by faith in the blood of an animal; the writer has already drawn the comparison between such blood and the power of the blood of the sinless Son of God.

11:29 'By faith they passed through the Red Sea as though they were passing through dry land; and the Egyptians, when they attempted it, were drowned.'

The Red Sea parted due to the effect of the wind that God sent at night while the angel of the Lord stood between the people and the Egyptian army. While the bed of the Red Sea was being dried out, hairdryer-style by the air movement, most of the Israelites would have been asleep. As Exodus (14:21) relates, 'The Lord swept the sea back by a strong east wind all night and turned the sea into dry land, so the waters were divided.' The Israelites had a choice to make; risk the walls of water collapsing or be annihilated by the pursuing army. They also had the choice of trusting in God's leadership as demonstrated by Moses or of giving up their hope of freedom. God created a sufficiently negative alternative so that they might trust in a humanly impossible one. This is mirrored in the gospel message. A humanly impossible option (God becoming man and dying on a Roman cross of execution) is offered against the option of dying in sin and entering the hell of eternal separation from God.

If '*pneuma*' is rendered with the well-recognised option of 'wind', instead of the more commonly used 'Spirit', then Jesus' statement to Nicodemus in John 3 carries a clear salvation lesson from Israel's history. John 3:4-5: 'Nicodemus said to him, "How can a man be born when he is old? He cannot enter a second time into his mother's womb and be born, can he?" Jesus answered, "Truly, truly, I say to you, unless one is born of water and the wind/Spirit he cannot enter into the kingdom of God."' Israel was birthed from slavery in Egypt into freedom in the Promised Land through the water and the wind, in separating and drying out the Red Sea to create firm ground on which to cross into Canaan.

11:30 'By faith the walls of Jericho fell down after they had been encircled for seven days.'

Joshua (6:1) records that 'Jericho was tightly shut because of the sons of Israel; no one went out and no one came in.' Jericho's walls were immense, being constructed as both an outer and an inner ring. The defeat of Jericho was a huge step forward militarily into the Promised Land, and one that was only possible to accomplish in such a short space of time with God's help. Once again, the people had to follow God's word to the letter. Joshua 6:2-6: 'The Lord said to Joshua, "See, I have given Jericho into your hand, with its king and the valiant warriors. You shall march around the city, all the men of war circling the city once. You shall do so for six days. Also seven priests shall carry seven trumpets of rams' horns before the ark; then on the seventh day you shall march around the city seven times, and the priests shall blow the trumpets. It shall be that when they make a long blast with the ram's horn, and when you hear the sound of the trumpet, all the people shall shout with a great shout; and the wall of the city will fall down flat, and the people will go up every man straight ahead."' The Hebrew of Joshua 6 records that the walls fell 'beneath themselves' i.e. 'flat', in other words they collapsed straight down, in itself a miraculous way of falling. They were not pushed over by the blast of a trumpet or by any human agency. The Israelite army could then go up over the rubble and into the city as God had commanded.

11:31 'By faith Rahab the harlot did not perish along with those who were disobedient, after she had welcomed the spies in peace.'

Rahab had harboured the Israelite spies and sent their pursuers on a false trail (Joshua 2:1-7). She lived in the city wall - how did she survive? German archaeologists Sellin and Watzinger excavated the site in 1907 and discovered a section of mud brick wall still standing to a height of eight feet with remains of housing attached. Rahab is attested to as a woman of faith. She had obeyed the word spoken to her to by the spies to 'tie this cord of scarlet thread in the window through which you let us down, and gather to yourself into the house your father and your mother and your brothers and all your father's household' (Joshua 2:18). This action on her part in trusting those instructions led to her safety and her part in the lineage of Messiah as the great-great-grandmother of King David (Matthew 1:5).

11:32 'And what more shall I say? For time will fail me if I tell of Gideon, Barak, Samson, Jephthah, of David and Samuel and the prophets.'

These men of faith all heard a word of instruction from God and obeyed it. Gideon had substantially reduced his army before engaging the Midianite enemy in battle. Barak, for all his timidity and reliance on Deborah's presence, had obeyed the word of the Lord through her and fought the superior numbers of the Canaanite army. Samson had (eventually, in a Philistine prison) returned to the sanctity of his Nazirite vow and fulfilled his mission of judgement against the lords of the Philistines. Jephthah, after accepting the offer of headship from the elders of Gilead, 'Spoke all his words before the Lord at Mizpah' (Judges 11:11). He was foolishly rash in the extreme (in his vow that led to the sacrifice of his daughter), but went from 'Before the Lord' and in a place of faith to subdue the Ammonites. David, Samuel and the many prophets all enjoyed close relationships with God, enabling them to hear from him and so actively respond in trust towards him.

11:33-34 'Who by faith conquered kingdoms, performed acts of righteousness, obtained promises, shut the mouths of lions, quenched the power of fire, escaped the edge of the sword, from weakness were made strong, became mighty in war, put foreign armies to flight.'

Joshua subdued the Canaanites and David conquered the Moabites, Syrians, Ammonites, and Edomites. They instituted God's reign based upon his word to Moses, the keeping of which was deemed as keeping 'righteousness' in God's eyes. Faith obtains what God has promised through trust and active obedience to his word (which does not always make logical sense to the limited human mind - e.g. Noah and the ark). David experienced God's faithfulness to his word in protecting him from lions when shepherding his father's flocks (1 Samuel 17:34); such protection would eventually be enjoyed on a more intense scale by the prophet Daniel (6:16-22). Daniel's friends Shadrach, Meshach and Abednego also experienced divine protection from King Nebuchadnezzar's fiery furnace (Daniel 3:16). Violent death ('the sword') was escaped by several of the prophets who had yet to fulfil all the will of God for their lives. Israel's kings were supposed to copy their own scroll of God's word (Deuteronomy 17:18) and obey it, as well as listening to the prophetic word; in so obeying they were able to deal supernaturally with opposing armies, as Elisha did with the Syrian army (2 Kings 6).

11:35-36 'Women received back their dead by resurrection; and others were tortured, not accepting their release, so that they might obtain a better resurrection; and others experienced mockings and scourgings, yes, also chains and imprisonment.'

Elijah restored her son to the woman of Zarephath, (1 Kings 17:19-22) and Elisha restored to life the son of the Shunammite woman (2 Kings 4:18-37). 'Tortured' here is '*tumpanizô*' (from which the word 'tympanic' is derived). Used of drums (the tympanic membrane is the ear drum), it means the beating of a stick against the skin of a person stretched tight over a wheel. Release on condition of renunciation of faith was rejected in the understanding that human life will always end; where we will spend eternity is in our own hands. 'Scourging' is a different Greek word, '*mastix*', (as in 'masticate' - 'to chew'). It is derived from '*masaomai*', meaning 'to chew and consume through direct contact', only in this case with human flesh. 'Mocking' is '*empaigmonê*', from '*paizô*', meaning 'to play with a child. Such were some of the hardships the people of God endured for their faith, and indeed many today still do so in regimes that are hostile to the Gospel.

11:37-38 'They were stoned, they were sawn in two, they were tempted, they were put to death with the sword; they went about in sheepskins, in goatskins, being destitute, afflicted, ill-treated, (men of whom the world was not worthy), wandering in deserts and mountains and caves and holes in the ground.'

Stoning was a common form of official and summary execution, as undergone by Zechariah the son of Jehoiada the priest (2 Chronicles 24:20-21). Isaiah is traditionally believed to have been sawn in two, having been discovered by King Manasseh hiding in a hollow tree, which was closed and hewn down with him inside it (Babylonian Talmud: Tractate Yebamoth 49). 'Tempted' ('*peirazô*' - testing, from '*peira*' - 'to experiment / make trial of') here probably means being tempted to deny their faith by various means of undue influence. Sometimes their faith led them to be rejected and ostracised, forced to live in the wild with only God to rely upon.

11:39-40 'And all these, having gained approval through their faith, did not receive what was promised, because God had provided something better for us, so that apart from us they would not be made perfect.'

The writer concludes his exposition on these old covenant examples of living faith by comparing the revelation they were living under with the 'better' provision that God had made in Christ. Without being joined to this, their faith, outstanding though it was, was 'incomplete' - not '*teleioô*' ('perfect'), because Christ, perfection personified, had not yet come. Only when the old dispensation of law was united with the new dispensation of grace and truth in Messiah, and the power of the Law to judge and condemn was broken by Messiah's death, would the perfect and complete will of Father God be manifest.

It is a sobering thing to compare these examples of those who possessed a not yet complete revelation of God's grace, with our own often timid lives. We have received the glorious and complete revelation of the Son of God and have been given the Holy Spirit. But do we lay hold of its fullness with passion and determination as they did? We need to 'step up to the plate' in order that our faith is worthy of theirs, so that their faith, along with ours, can be perfected. May God strengthen us to do just that.

Chapter 12

Come to Jesus, the mediator of a new covenant

12:1 'Therefore, since we have so great a cloud of witnesses surrounding us, let us also lay aside every encumbrance and the sin which so easily entangles us, and let us run with endurance the race that is set before us.'

The Christian life is likened to a race with the old covenant saints as cheering on-lookers. The witnesses are now in heaven as spiritual beings (hence 'cloud', or 'vapour'), and are therefore unencumbered by weight, both natural and spiritual. 'Encumbrance' is '***ogkos***', meaning (excess) 'weight' or 'bulk' which long-distance runners avoid. In the Greek games runners would run naked ('gymnasium' comes from the Greek '***gumnos***', meaning 'naked'); the writer encourages his readers to run without the impediment of excess baggage and sin. It is easy to take on burdens that the race Organiser never intended for us to bear. John wrote that 'His commandments are not burdensome' (1 John 5:3), yet it is easy to make them so. The race is a long-distance one, hence 'endurance' ('patience') is needed.

12:2 'Fixing our eyes on Jesus, the author and perfecter of faith, who for the joy set before him endured the cross, despising the shame, and has sat down at the right hand of the throne of God.'

Races need an end-point to aim towards; ours is the person of Christ himself. Jesus takes our fledgling faith and brings it to full-grown completion, if we let him through our active cooperation. 'Author' here is '***archêgos***', also meaning 'One that takes the lead in anything and thus affords an example'. [39] Jesus modelled for us what living a life of faith means - complete dependency on his Father for the word of guidance that he needed in order to be doing his Father's will. If anyone could justify independent behaviour it was the Son of God, however Jesus modelled dependency - he only said and did the things he saw his Father say and do. [xxxv] Jesus 'finishes' our faith in the sense of bringing it to a perfect completion, again, provided we cooperate with him. Once he has begun something he promises to finish it (Philippians 1:6: 'He who began a good work in you will perfect it until the day of Christ Jesus').

Jesus also provides an example of the long-distance 'endurance' needed all the way to Calvary. The writer uses another word for 'endured' to that in verse one - '*hupomenô*' - 'to remain under'. Jesus could have called upon twelve legions (12,000) angels to deliver him from his arrest in the Garden of Gethsemane (Matthew 26:53). Instead he voluntarily chose to 'remain under' what he knew to be his Father's will for him. The 'shame' is '*aischunê*', also meaning 'disgrace' - the disgrace of dying a degrading criminal's death, a disgrace made all the more 'shameful' by his having been a senior Torah teacher subject to a death sentence for alleged blasphemy. Jesus is truly worthy to re-take his seat at the Father's right-hand, only this time with the reward of his faithfulness.

12:3 'For consider him who has endured such hostility by sinners against himself, so that you will not grow weary and lose heart.'

'Endured' is again '*hupomenô*', in this case choosing to 'remain under' the hostility of sinful men and women. The second person of

---

[xxxv] "Truly, truly, I say to you, the Son can do nothing of himself, unless it is something he sees the Father doing; for whatever, the Father does, these things the Son also does in like manner" (John 5:19).

the triune God was legally entitled to receive respect and obedience; Jesus put up with a lot of the exact opposite type of behaviour from his creation, to whom he had magnanimously granted freewill. Jesus' good example of patience is supposed to inspire us to imitate his life of choosing to lean on his Father and draw from him the strength needed to tolerate sinful men without giving up on them. Without such imitation of him we will be likely to tire ('become enfeebled', or 'weary') in our 'souls' (*'psuche'*). 'Heart' is *'kardia'*, the Greek rendered as 'heart' in this verse is in fact 'soul' - the place of our spiritual breath that keeps us alive. Long-distance runners need to maintain their wind, and discouragement ('running out of puff' spiritually) is a key way that the devil will cause loss of race participation. Helping with 'giving up' is one of his specialities.

The disciple should expect at some point to share their Master's lot; Jesus had made that clear to his followers. 'A slave is not greater than his master. If they persecuted me they will also persecute you' (John 15:20). Only that which God permits for our strengthening can happen under the Father's direction. He knows perfectly what we are capable of bearing and only allows trials to serve for our eventual good. James, who was martyred for his faith in his half-brother Jesus, could say, 'Count it all joy, my brethren, when you encounter various trials, knowing that the testing of your faith produces endurance.' So God-sent trials (as opposed to burdens we put upon ourselves) are an important part of the spiritual long-distance runners' training programme.

12:4-6 'You have not yet resisted to the point of shedding blood in your striving against sin; and you have forgotten the exhortation which is addressed to you as sons: "My son, do not regard lightly the discipline of the Lord, nor faint when you are reproved by him; for those whom the Lord loves he disciplines, and he scourges every son whom he receives."'

The writer quotes Proverbs 3:11-12, 'My son, do not reject the discipline of the Lord, or loathe his reproof, for whom the Lord loves he reproves, even as a father corrects the son in whom he delights.' 'Discipline' is intended to be a source of strength, just as pruning a vine ensures healthier growth. The Greek here (on both occasions in verses 5 and 6) is '*paideia*', meaning 'the whole training and education of children, including appropriate chastisement.' [40] 'Reprove' ('*elegchô*') has to do with conviction of sin. 'Scourges' is '*mastigoô*', the Jewish form of the punishment (as opposed to the Roman '*flagellum*' with its bone and metal implants). Unlike the Roman version a '*mastigoô*' spread the beating's impact between both shoulders and the back. The writer is quoting in verse 6 from the Greek translation of the Hebrew Old Testament proverb, the Hebrew of which reads '*yakach*', meaning 'reprove and correct'. [41]

The Jews followed the practice of physical discipline both in correcting and punishing children (Proverbs 23:13-14, a 'rod' - '*shebet*' - in this context is a 'small branch', or 'off-shoot') and to a lesser extent in training children in obedience (Proverbs 22:15). The discipline / reproof administered in love is to steer us away from the much more harmful thing called sin. Paul used the same term in connection with reproving the Church at Corinth ('Shall I come to you with a rod?' - 1 Corinthians 4:21).

12:7-9 'It is for discipline that you endure; God deals with you as with sons; for what son is there whom his father does not discipline? But if you are without discipline, of which all have become partakers, then you are illegitimate children and not sons. Furthermore, we had earthly fathers to discipline us, and we respected them; shall we not much rather be subject to the Father of spirits, and live?'

The correction and discipline that we receive are signs to us of God's fatherly care. Those left without discipline are illegitimate (Greek: '***nothos***' - 'bastard'); they often end up with behavioural problems due to inadequate or ineffectual parenting. 'Respect' is '***entrepo***', which when used as here in the Greek as the passive voice means 'to show deference and reverent respect'. [42] The end result is eternal life, (Greek: '***zaô***' - 'to be alive') just as honouring and respecting parents leads to life as the fifth commandment states (Exodus 20:12). [xxxvi] 'Subject to' is '***hupotassô***' ('place under'); God calls us to place ourselves voluntarily under his Fatherly hand and receive the benefits of his heavenly parenting skills. God does not force obedience, but his lovingly invoked parental discipline will certainly follow wilful disobedience.

12:10-11 'For they disciplined us for a short time as seemed best to them, but he disciplines us for our good, so that we may share his holiness. All discipline for the moment seems not to be joyful, but sorrowful; yet to those who have been trained by it, afterwards it yields the peaceful fruit of righteousness.'

The correction and appropriate chastisement of children necessarily only occurs for the 'short time' of their childhood. God's discipline allows us to more closely share in his nature by steering us away from sin and towards godliness. 'Sorrowful' is '***lupê***', the sorrow associated with pain and grief, in this case the grief that our sin causes God to feel and that sense of his pain that we should share in when we sin. The writer now brings the theme back to running a race with his use of the word 'trained'. It is '***gumnazô***' - 'to vigorously exercise', again, from '***gumnos***', meaning 'naked', from which we

---

[xxxvi] Exodus 20:12: 'Honour your father and your mother, that your days may be prolonged in the land which the Lord your God gives you.'

derive the word 'gymnasium'. God trains us for our eternal benefit, in order that we might bear fruit in this life that will endure through to the next. The intended consequence is that this will ultimately yield a harvest of right behaviour ('righteousness') that honours God. The fruit is 'peaceful'; it also reflects the other attributes of the work of the Holy Spirit in our lives (Galatians 5:22-23). [xxxvii] By such fruits Jesus' followers are recognised (Matthew 7:18-20). [xxxviii]

12:12-13 'Therefore, strengthen the hands that are weak and the knees that are feeble, and make straight paths for your feet, so that the limb which is lame may not be put out of joint, but rather be healed.'

Maintaining his theme of vigorous exercise, the writer (quoting Proverbs 4:26, 'Make level paths for your feet') encourages the 'strengthening' ('lifting to set straight') of weak hands and 'feeble' (literally 'palsied') knees, and to run in a 'straight' way. This is the way that John the Baptist described the coming of God's kingdom and preparing the 'way of the Lord' (Luke 3:4-5). 'Paths' is *'trochia'*, meaning the compressed earth left behind by the wheels of a chariot. Lameness of limbs needs strengthening ('making whole') before it leads to dislocation. This divine physiotherapy and spiritual training involves the exercise of our faith, in hearing from God and obeying his word to us in a disposition of trust and reliance on him. This is 'faith working through love' (Galatians 5:6). Paul could say (2 Corinthians 12:10) that he was 'Well content with weaknesses, with insults, with distresses, with persecutions, with difficulties, for

---

[xxxvii] Galatians 5:22-23: 'The fruit of the Spirit is love, joy, peace, patience, kindness, goodness, faithfulness, gentleness, self-control; against such things there is no law.'

[xxxviii] Matthew 7:18-20: 'A good tree cannot produce bad fruit, nor can a bad tree produce good fruit. Every tree that does not bear good fruit is cut down and thrown into the fire. So then, you will know them by their fruits.'

Christ's sake, for when I am weak then I am strong.' He knew that such hardships threw him in ever-greater dependence onto God, the source of supernatural strength that specialises in doing that which for men is impossible.

12:14 'Pursue peace with all men, and the sanctification without which no one will see the Lord.'

The racing analogies continue with 'pursue' ('***diôkô***'), meaning 'to run swiftly in order to catch up with a person.' [43] The object of all this spiritual exercise is to cooperate with God's restoration of the family likeness in us, and to grow in the exercise of our faith muscles. 'Peace' is the tranquility of '***eirênê***', doubtless the author had the Hebrew '***shalom***' in mind, meaning a completeness of wholeness and well-being. The subsequent godliness will allow others to see the Lord in us. This process of sanctification is part of the second stage of '***sozo***' ('salvation') in the on-going sense of the present-continuous tense in which the verb is used. We have been saved, we are being saved and we will be saved. That the second part is happening is evidence to us and everyone else that the first part had occurred and that the third will follow, when we receive our new and incorruptible body upon arrival in heaven.

12:15-17 'See to it that no one comes short of the grace of God; that no root of bitterness springing up causes trouble, and by it many be defiled; that there be no immoral or godless person like Esau, who sold his own birthright for a single meal. For you know that even afterwards, when he desired to inherit the blessing, he was rejected, for he found no place for repentance, though he sought for it with tears.'

The 'race' theme continues apace with '***hustereô***' ('coming short' or 'to be left behind in the race and so fail to reach the goal'). [44] God's grace and unmerited favour is what enables us to maintain the attitude of faith and so to continue to draw upon God's strength as dependent entirely upon that and not upon ourselves and our own strengths. The result of self-reliance rather than God-reliance will be a bitter fruit ('root' is '***rhiza***', also meaning an 'off-shoot') rather than the 'peaceful' Holy Spirit generated fruit of verse 11. These shoots 'spring up' to cause 'trouble' rather than peace. The result is the 'off-colour tinge' of 'defilement'. '***Miainô***' ('defiled') is the term used here for the colour contamination or staining that could occur in the process of dyeing cloth, thus spoiling the garment in a way that the designer never intended.

'Immoral' here is the term for a male prostitute or fornicator; 'godless' is 'profane' as opposed to what is sacred. Esau was such a person; he took many foreign wives (Genesis 36:2) and he despised his father and his father's inheritance to the point of selling it for a simple meal of bread and lentil stew (Genesis 25:34). Once Isaac had given his blessing to Jacob (whether knowingly or not) it was not to be revoked; despite all of Esau's pleading to his father, only a much lesser blessing was forthcoming (Genesis 27:39-40).

12:18-21 'For you have not come to a mountain that can be touched and to a blazing fire, and to darkness and gloom and whirlwind, and to the blast of a trumpet and the sound of words which sound was such that those who heard begged that no further word be spoken to them. For they could not bear the command, 'If even a beast touches the mountain, it will be stoned.' And so terrible was the sight, that Moses said, "I am full of fear and trembling."'

The writer now switches away from his 'race' theme to look back at the giving of the Law to Moses on Mount Sinai, and the associated regulations as recorded in Exodus 19:10-13. The command from God at that time was to sanctify the mountain by commanding that the people stay away on pain of death. The accompanying signs of God's arrival (Exodus 19:18-19 - trumpet, fire, earthquake and thunder), and the giving of God's Law (words the sound of which engendered trepidation in the hearers) caused fear and awe in the on-lookers, including Moses himself ('I feared the anger and wrath of the Lord' Deuteronomy 9:19, NIV). There is a right fear of God that is 'the beginning of wisdom' (Proverbs 9:10). It is this type of fear towards God that builds a healthy respect which brings about a disposition of obedience in the lives of those who practice it.

12:22-24 'But you have come to Mount Zion and to the city of the living God, the heavenly Jerusalem, and to myriads of angels, to the general assembly and church of the firstborn who are enrolled in heaven, and to God, the Judge of all, and to the spirits of the righteous made perfect, and to Jesus, the mediator of a new covenant, and to the sprinkled blood, which speaks better than the blood of Abel.'

The writer contrasts Mount Sinai to Mount Zion, on which was built the Temple where God dwelled on earth, being symbolic of his residence in heaven, the eternal city of the New Jerusalem. The 'assembly' ('*panêguris*' - 'a festal gathering', such as accompanied the Greek races the writer mentions) and the 'church' ('*ekklêsia*', meaning 'a gathering of called-out citizens') transcends time and space between earth and heaven, being spiritually connected. Amazingly, the writer tells us that 'You have come' to all that he describes, not 'You will come'. We are now citizens of heaven seated with Christ in heavenly places, an amazing honour which God bestows on us.

Jesus is the 'firstborn of all creation', and it is his eternal 'gathering' ('*ekklêsia*') into which God draws all those that he has 'enrolled' ('*apographo*' - 'those written down in the public record'). Jesus encouraged his disciples to 'rejoice that their names are recorded in heaven' (Luke 10:20). There countless angels dwell amongst the saints who have gained their reward, and there God the Father sits enthroned with Jesus, whose incarnation meant that God and man were brought back into fellowship following the estrangement that Adam's sin had brought. Jesus' shed blood, 'sprinkled' in heaven, meant that the dispensation of mercy, grace and truth could be inaugurated, a much better testimony to God's nature than the blood of Abel, that only called out for vengeance for his wrongful death.

12:25-27 'See to it that you do not refuse him who is speaking. For if those did not escape when they refused him who warned them on earth, much less will we escape who turn away from him who warns from heaven. And his voice shook the earth then, but now he has promised, saying, "Yet once more I will shake not only the earth, but also the heaven." This expression, 'Yet once more' denotes the removing of those things which can be shaken, as of created things, so that those things which cannot be shaken may remain.'

The writer issues a stern warning to his audience to pay much more attention to the consequences of Jesus' sacrifice than they had to the giving of the Law to Moses. They had valued that above all; now, the writer says, there is something much greater. Once again, the importance of listening, in faith, to God is emphasised as the means to stability. As Psalm 119:165 says, 'Those who love your '*torah*' ('word' or 'Law') have great peace, nothing causes them to stumble.' The writer quotes from Haggai 2, verse 6: 'This is what the Lord Almighty says: "In a little while I will once more shake the heavens and the earth, the sea and the dry land."' The heavens will indeed shake at the return of Christ, when "There will be signs in sun and moon and stars, and on the earth dismay among nations, in perplexity at the roaring of the sea and the waves, men fainting from fear and the expectation of the things which are coming upon the world; for the powers of the heavens will be shaken. Then they will see the Son of Man coming in a cloud with power and great glory" (Luke 21:25-27). And as the Apostle John saw, 'A great white throne and him who sat upon it, from whose presence earth and heaven fled away' (Revelation 20:11). Heaven itself cannot be shaken, it will remain, and God will create re-create 'A new heaven and a new earth; for the first heaven and the first earth passed away' (Revelation 21:1). The Kingdom of Heaven can never be shaken.

12:28-29 'Therefore, since we receive a kingdom which cannot be shaken, let us show gratitude, by which we may offer to God an acceptable service with reverence and awe; for our God is a consuming fire.

'Gratitude' is indeed the appropriate response to God's most-gracious intervention in the despair and death-filled world of sin that mankind inhabits. However the Greek here reads '***echô charis***' - 'have grace' (as in the KJV). The writer closes this section with the thought that to avoid becoming like Esau, we need to have the grace that Esau came up short of in his particular race of life. That grace enables us to lean onto God and so live in the attitude of 'trust' that God finds acceptable and pleasing, for 'Without faith it is impossible to please God' (Hebrews 11:6).

The word translated as 'reverence' here is '***aidôs***', from '***aideomai***' - 'to be ashamed', [45] which is only used in one other place in the New Testament, in 1 Timothy 2:9. Here Paul tells the women of Ephesus, 'I want women to adorn themselves with proper clothing, with modesty and discretion' - 'modesty' here is '***aidôs***'. The fact that the writer to the Hebrews couples his use of the term with 'awe' ('***eulabeia***' - 'godly fear' or 'reverence') indicates that 'modesty' is the more likely rendering (rather than 'reverence'), because he is unlikely to have used two terms for exactly the same thing in describing how our service of God is to be. 'Modesty' is an extremely helpful attribute for the believer to have in respect of their service towards God. Such service is done with the gifts that God himself has given, however it is all too easy to take credit for it, credit that actually belongs to God himself. The works of the flesh are headed for the fire of judgement (of our works - 1 Corinthians 3:12) and God himself will not tolerate his glory being given to another (Isaiah 42:8). All such dead works will be utterly consumed by fire; none will pass on into eternity, whereas the inheritance that God has for his children is 'Imperishable and undefiled and will not fade away, reserved in heaven for us' (1 Peter 1:4).

Chapter 13

Jesus - Forever the Same

13:1-3 'Let love of the brethren continue. Do not neglect to show hospitality to strangers, for by this some have entertained angels without knowing it. Remember the prisoners, as though in prison with them, and those who are ill-treated, since you yourselves also are in the body.'

The writer concludes his letter with a collection of different points. The first is the need for '***philadelphia***' - 'brotherly love'. Care of the faith community, now an often-persecuted minority, was paramount. As Paul said to the Galatian church community (6:10): 'While we have opportunity, let us do good to all people, and especially to those who are of the household of the faith.' There was a strong cultural norm around hospitality, and faith in Messiah did not obviate this. The patriarch Abraham was following the normal pattern of behaviour within his culture when he prepared food for his three visitors while he was lodging at the oaks of Mamre (Genesis 18:1). What he did not realise was that one of them was named 'Yahweh' ('the Lord', the pre-incarnate second Person of the trinity); the other two were angels (Genesis 19:1) sent to execute judgement against Sodom and Gomorrah.

The 'prisoners' are 'in bonds' as Paul describes himself as being in Colossians 4:18. The concept of identifying with how one's brethren are treated, as if being so treated oneself is typical of covenanted groups such as families and households. It is this principle that Paul put forward in writing to the Corinthians, 'If one member suffers, all the members suffer with it; if one member is honoured, all the members rejoice with it' (1 Corinthians 12:26), and 'That the members may have the same care for one another' (1 Corinthians

12:25). Jesus taught that what one person did to those of his people in need ('The least of these brothers of mine') is also done to him (Matthew 25:34-45).

13:4 'Marriage is to be held in honour among all, and the marriage bed is to be undefiled; for fornicators and adulterers God will judge.'

Celibacy was practiced by the extremely devout Jewish community of the Essenes, with whom Jesus was familiar ('They neglect wedlock').[46] The house in which the last supper was held was almost certainly a celibate Essene residence, given the highly unusual meeting scenario of a man carrying water (Luke 22:10). Jesus was celibate; and Paul upheld it as a 'better' state than marriage in light of the 'undivided devotion' it can bring in terms of serving God (1 Corinthians 7:35 and 38). The writer balances any disparaging treatment from the celibates by stressing the God-ordained nature of marriage as a vocation and call from God. Paul did the same, 'Each man has his own gift from God, one in this manner, and another, in that' (1 Corinthians 7:7). God has 'sanctified' ('made holy') sexual relations ('the marriage bed') within marriage and wants them to be protected from corrupt sexual practices such as fornication and adultery. Those who do such things will be subject to '*krinô*', meaning 'Separated out for judgement',[47] just as the goats are separated from the sheep after Jesus' return (Matthew 25:33). God encourages pastoral care that will 'restore such a one in the spirit of gentleness', while at the same time 'looking to yourself that you too will not be tempted' (Galatians 6:1). We are to 'have mercy with fear, hating even the garment spotted by the flesh' (Jude 23), 'avoiding even the appearance of evil' (1 Thessalonians 5:22).

13:5-6 'Make sure that your character is free from the love of money, being content with what you have; for he himself has said, "I will never desert you, nor will I ever

forsake you", so that we confidently say, "The Lord is my helper, I will not be afraid, what will man do to me?"'

Love of money is fundamentally a form of idolatry, and one that betrays a lack of trust in God to provide for one's needs. God's fatherly presence with us means that he is committed to meeting our every need. That does not obviate our own need to work, but rather means that work should be done in an attitude of God-dependency rather than self-dependency. Throughout the Old Testament God is identified as the 'helper' of his people. The writer uses the word '***boêthos***', from '***boê***', meaning 'to cry'. God waits for his people to cry out to him. He is not at all averse to leaving things until the last minute, when need has turned into desperation and we call out to him for help.

God's sovereignty as King of the universe means that we can trust in his complete control over the things that happen to us, with the power to turn all things to our good, even the most unpalatable, such as the oppression that the early Church was facing. Man's hostility could go up to the limits of what God permitted and no further, and martyrdom carried an eternal crown of reward. The writer quotes from Deuteronomy 31:6, where Moses encouraged the people of Israel to enter the Promised Land with the words 'The Lord will never leave you or forsake you.' He then quotes Psalm 118:6 - 'The Lord is for me, I will not fear; what can man do to me?', with a boldness that comes from meditating on the word and inwardly appropriating it in faith and trust. The fear of the Lord more than cancels out the fear of men; it leads to a holy boldness to pursue the will of God whatever people may say or think.

13:7 'Remember those who led you, who spoke the word of God to you; and considering the result of their conduct, imitate their faith.'

The use of the past tense indicates that the writer is following-up his thoughts about 'What men could do' with a reference to those who had already paid the ultimate price of discipleship to the One who had been nailed to a Roman stake of execution. Such men included the first martyr Stephen and James, brother of John. They had faithfully passed on Christ's teaching and ultimately his example of servanthood unto death - 'the result of their conduct'. The Greek here is '***ekbasis anastrophē***', also meaning the 'end of life'. The believers are called to 'mimic' ('imitate', from '***mimos***' - 'a mimic') their faith, in trust in the God who will lead them to whatever the best possible outcome for them is, in relationship with him. In our self-centred culture, with its prideful boast of 'Nobody tells me what to do, I'm going to be myself', few understand that all that means is being a meaningless clone of every other 'rebel'. Imitating the example of the godly in their faith and relationship with God will lead to true freedom and a genuine discovery of who we are destined to be in God. Having the humility to imitate them is integral to this.

13:8 'Jesus Christ is the same yesterday and today and forever.'

Jesus' eternal nature is unchanging. Hence death could not hold him, for he was Life itself in bodily form. His bodily death in willing subjection to his Father's will did not remove from him 'The power of an indestructible life' (consistent with Melchizedek - Hebrews 7:16). Jesus' resurrection means that he is the same person to us today as he was for the twelve apostles, the same leader and the same guide. Jesus never changed his nature, nor could he, being eternally the second Person of the triune God.

13:9 'Do not be carried away by varied and strange teachings; for it is good for the heart to be strengthened by grace, not by foods, through which those who were so occupied were not benefited.'

The idea of Jesus' holiness being changed on the cross and the triunity of the Godhead being consequently broken could be a good example of a 'divers' or 'varied' (*'poililos'* - 'different coloured') doctrine that is *'xenos'* ('foreign') to the Scripture as a whole and to the very nature of God. The Jew's dietary regulations were a key part of the Jewish Oral Law and consequently their legal understanding of holiness, but they had not profited the people spiritually. On the contrary they had led to pride and a Rabbinically-added burden that God never intended the people to bear. Such burdens as the Oral Law's commands regarding the Sabbath led to Jesus' statement that 'The Sabbath was for man, and not man for the Sabbath' (Mark 2:27). The Oral Law led to a high degree of focus upon the Rabbi's traditions ('Precepts of men' - Mark 7:7) rather than upon the God who had given the original commandments to Moses. The main benefit of the Law was to show men and women that God's standards (reflected by it) were not something that they could attain of their own strength.

13:10-11 'We have an altar from which those who serve the tabernacle have no right to eat. For the bodies of those animals whose blood is brought into the holy place by the high priest as an offering for sin, are burned outside the camp.'

The altar referred to is the one in heaven at which Jesus poured out his own blood, in a holy and acceptable atonement for the sins of the world, past, present and future. The priests were legally entitled to eat of some of the offerings the people made (Leviticus 10:14). [xxxix] Such a privileged position has no bearing upon their partaking of Christ's heavenly offering, which is received by faith and trust in

---

[xxxix] 'The breast of the wave offering, however, and the thigh of the offering you may eat in a clean place, you and your sons and your daughters with you' (Leviticus 10:14).

him and his sacrifice of himself at Calvary. Only by joining the community of faith can one partake of the meal that accompanies the sacrifice of the Lord Jesus Christ. As Jesus said, 'My flesh is true food, and my blood is true drink. He who eats my flesh and drinks my blood abides in me, and I in him' (John 6:55-56). Burned offerings for sin were indeed burned utterly outside the camp of the people of Israel, and outside the gates of Jerusalem after temple offerings replaced the tabernacle in the time of King Solomon. Their carcases were not eaten of at all, rather they were consumed by fire.

13:12-13 'Therefore Jesus also, that he might sanctify the people through his own blood, suffered outside the gate. So, let us go out to him outside the camp, bearing his reproach.'

Jesus fulfils the law of the burnt offering by dying outside the gate of Jerusalem, and his blood provides a permanent source of purification for sin, one that needs no repetition. The excommunication that the curse of his 'death on a tree' (Deuteronomy 21:23) brought him was one mirrored within the community of Messianic believers once the wider Jewish community closed ranks against it. 'Reproach' ('*oneidismos*') carries the meaning of being 'defamed and reviled', which the early Jewish believers experienced. They were seen as being disciples of a perceived and cursed apostate by Jews, and by the Romans as pagans who performed a type of blood sacrifice in the mis-portrayed communion service. They truly experienced 'the fellowship of Jesus' sufferings' (Philippians 3:10).

13:14 'For here we do not have a lasting city, but we are seeking the city which is to come.'

The city of Jerusalem (outside of which Jesus suffered) was but a pale and temporary shadow of the true city of God in heaven itself. In just a few years time it would be destroyed by the Roman army under Vespasian. By contrast, the 'lasting' city is the new Jerusalem of Revelation 21:1-2. 'I saw a new heaven and a new earth; for the first heaven and the first earth passed away, and there is no longer any sea. And I saw the holy city, new Jerusalem, coming down out of heaven from God, made ready as a bride adorned for her husband.' The writer returns to the example of the patriarch Abraham, whom, he has said in chapter 11 verse 16, was 'Longing for a better country - a heavenly one. Therefore God is not ashamed to be called their God, for he has prepared a city for them.'

13:15 'Through him then, let us continually offer up a sacrifice of praise to God, that is, the fruit of lips that give thanks to his name.'

Sacrifices are not quite done with though - there remains the 'Sacrifice of praise'. King David had sacrificed 'freewill offerings', 'I will freely sacrifice unto thee: I will praise thy name, O Lord; for it is good' (Psalms 54:6 KJV). We are invited to come before God not with the Levitical law's fourth year fruit of the field (Leviticus 19:24), but rather with the 'Fruit of the lips' that the prophet Hosea had spoken of. 'Return, O Israel, to the Lord your God, for you have stumbled because of your iniquity. Take words with you and return to the Lord. Say to him, "Take away all iniquity, and receive us graciously, that we may present the fruit of our lips"' (Hosea 14:1-2).

13:16 'And do not neglect doing good and sharing, for with such sacrifices God is pleased.'

Giving to others constituted an acceptable sacrifice (if performed in faith) in the alms-giving of the Old Covenant, and God still regards such offerings as acceptable. 'Sharing' here is '*koinônia*', the contributory fellowship that the Macedonian (largely Gentile) saints had set such store by in demonstrating their equality in New Covenant standing to the Judean Jewish believers. 2 Corinthians

8:1-5: 'Now, brethren, we wish to make known to you the grace of God which has been given in the churches of Macedonia, that in a great ordeal of affliction their abundance of joy and their deep poverty overflowed in the wealth of their liberality. For I testify that according to their ability, and beyond their ability, they gave of their own accord, begging us with much urging for the favour of participation in the support of the saints, and this, not as we had expected, but they first gave themselves to the Lord and to us by the will of God.' Such sacrifices are truly 'acceptable' ('*euaresteô*' - 'pleasing', from '*euarestos*' - 'acceptable'). If we truly understood that God is 'pleased' with such giving perhaps we would give more liberally, more generously, more gladly. If we could learn to love God's smile of approval more than our treasures and possessions, a river of supply would be released to the needy and broken and to the missionary purpose of the church.

13:17 'Obey your leaders and submit to them, for they keep watch over your souls as those who will give an account. Let them do this with joy and not with grief, for this would be unprofitable for you.'

While God does require obedience to his word, the passage here does not actually say 'obey' (which is '*hupakoê*' - as in Philemon 1:21, 'Having confidence in your obedience, I write to you, since I know that you will do even more than what I say'). Rather the writer uses the word '*peithô*', meaning 'To be persuaded by something so as to have confidence in it', or 'To win over'. [48] Because the church operates on a voluntary basis, the leadership needs to have the full confidence of their members through persuasive example and words of direction that inspire confidence. The church members can then be 'persuaded' that what they are being asked to do is of God. In addition, 'submit' rendered here is not the usual '*hupotassô*' ('To place under', e.g. in regard to legitimate authority), but rather '*hupeikô*', meaning 'To yield' to them when possible. Leaders will give 'an accounting' for the '***psuchê***' ('souls' and also meaning 'lives') of those that they watch over; making life difficult for them in this regard is counter-productive for the ones being watched over. 'Grief' here is '***stenazô***', meaning 'To complain with a loud sigh'; something that is a sad alternative to the '***chara***' ('rejoicing') that is supposed to accompany their ministry.

13:18-19 'Pray for us, for we are sure that we have a good conscience, desiring to conduct ourselves honourably in all things. And I urge you all the more to do this, so that I may be restored to you the sooner.'

Rather than adopt a position of spiritual superiority as a 'leader', the writer humbles himself and asks for their prayers. He has a good conscience, but knows that this by itself is not a guarantee of freedom from 'hidden faults'. (Who can discern his errors? Acquit me of hidden faults - Psalms 19:12.) 'Honourable' is '***kalôs***', which carries the meaning of 'honesty' and 'blamelessness', [49] something that today's leaders would do well to bear in mind in a money-oriented society. 'Restored' has been taken by some scholars to allude to the writer's imprisonment and hence to Paul as a possible author, however '***apokathistêmi***' equally well means 'To restore to health' [50] (e.g. Mark 3:5) [xl] or 'returned', e.g. in the case of the kingdom of Israel (Acts 1:6). [xli] The reference to 'coming with Timothy' who has 'just been released' from prison (verse 23) mitigates against a prison reference on the part of the writer, who is clearly at liberty to accompany Timothy to see those to whom he is writing.

[xl] 'Jesus said to the man, "Stretch out your hand." And he stretched it out, and his hand was *restored*'('***apokathistêmi***' - Mark 3:5).

[xli] 'Lord, is it at this time you are *restoring* ('***apokathistêmi***') the kingdom to Israel?' (Acts 1:6).

13:20-21 'Now the God of peace, who brought up from the dead the great Shepherd of the sheep through the blood of the eternal covenant, even Jesus our Lord, equip you in every good thing to do his will, working in us that which is pleasing in his sight, through Jesus Christ, to whom be the glory forever and ever. Amen.'

The writer's closing blessing evokes the peace of God's *'shalom'* wholeness, exhibited in restoring Christ from the dead to his rightful place at the Father's side. Jesus' resurrection power, his covenant keeping faithfulness, and the new life that his blood-sacrifice made possible are all available to make his children complete and equipped to serve him. Doing the Father's will is the responsibility of all mature children. It is up to us to 'Learn what is pleasing to the Lord' (Ephesians 5:10), and to seek out both him and his will for us in our service of him, moving in faith and trust into the 'good works, which God prepared beforehand so that we would walk in them' (Ephesians 2:10). God will work his will out 'in us' as we 'Trust in him with all our hearts, and do not lean on our own understanding' (Proverbs 3:5). Jesus' 'glory' ('*doxa*') was powerfully manifest in his own doing of his Father's will to the uttermost. '*Doxa*' comes from '*dokeô*', which means how someone is 'thought of', in the sense of their 'reputation'.

Jesus 'made himself of no reputation' in his incarnation in comparison with his status within the triune God. 'He made himself of no reputation, and took upon him the form of a servant, and was made in the likeness of men. And being found in fashion as a man, he humbled himself, and became obedient unto death, even the death of the cross. Wherefore God also hath highly exalted him, and given him a name which is above every name, that at the name of Jesus every knee should bow, of things in heaven, and things in earth, and things under the earth, and that every tongue should confess that Jesus Christ is Lord, to the glory of God the Father' (Philippians 2:7-

11, KJV). Jesus now has a reputation 'Above every name', based not just on his divine status and nature but also on what his mission accomplished for mankind. The church and the individual believer are to now go about making the One who is good, look good, to a watching world.

13:22-23 'But I urge you, brethren, bear with this word of exhortation, for I have written to you briefly. Take notice that our brother Timothy has been released, with whom, if he comes soon, I will see you.'

'Exhortation' here is '*paraklêsis*', from '*parakaleô*', meaning 'To call alongside to help', this being the work of the Holy Spirit. It is commonly translated as 'consolation' and that is the essence of what the writer has been offering to the believers now estranged from the mainstream Jewish faith. Timothy, like Paul, had been imprisoned but was now apparently free to accompany the writer.

13:24-25 'Greet all of your leaders and all the saints. Those from Italy greet you. Grace be with you all.'

Final greetings are offered to the whole community of faith; those in leadership and the entire body of the '*hagios*'. These are 'holy ones' by virtue of being set apart for God and the new life of God that had been gifted to them by the unmerited favour ('grace') that the writer commends them to. The writer appears to have been writing from Italy, and sends the greetings of the local believers with his own.

Who Wrote Hebrews And When?

There are several theories regarding the author of Hebrews.

1) Paul wrote it. This is highly unlikely for the following reasons:

    a) The Greek style and quality of the prose is completely different to Paul's, being of a much more literary style. The writer appears to be writing or dictating in his first language, and the letter's introduction (Chapter 1:1-3) ranks among the finest and most fluent Greek in the New Testament. Paul's writings tended to follow a Hebrew non-linear pattern, in contrast to the step-wise approach taken by the book's author.
    b) The writer uses a Greek oratory style, similar to Greek philosophers such as Demosthenes. [51] Paul was no orator. He acknowledges this clearly in 2 Corinthians 11:6 ('I am not a trained speaker') and his audience of Greek philosophers in Athens derided him as an 'idle babbler' ('*spermologos*', meaning 'One who passes on scraps of knowledge' - Acts 17:18).
    c) The writer quotes from the Septuagint (the Greek version of the Old Testament), whereas Paul, a disciple of the Bet Midrash school of Gamaliel, extensively used the Hebrew texts.
    d) The letter lacks Paul's typical opening statement of authorship as well as his typical closing personal greeting.
    e) The writer was at liberty to speak of accompanying Timothy who had recently been released from prison (Hebrews 13:23); Timothy is spoken of as a peer and not as a son, as was Paul's custom (1 Timothy 1:2 and 18).

f) The writer to the Hebrews is passing on his teaching as a non-eyewitness of Christ (Hebrews 2:3 - 'Confirmed unto us by them that heard him'). Paul (a Temple scholar under Gamaliel) would have been exposed to Jesus' Temple ministry and so have 'heard him' teach over a period of years. Furthermore Paul affirms that he received the gospel from Christ himself (Galatians 1:12, [xlii] and 1 Corinthians 15:8). [xliii]

2) Apollos wrote it. 'Now there was a Jew named Apollos, an Alexandrian by birth, an eloquent man... and he was mighty in the Scriptures... and fervent in spirit, he was speaking and teaching accurately the things concerning Jesus... demonstrating by the Scriptures that Jesus was the Christ' (Acts 18:24 and 28). Apollos was a Greek orator, from Alexandria, the city founded by Alexander the Great. As such he is the best placed of all the known New Testament candidates to have been responsible for the fine-flowing Greek prose of chapter 1. Like Barnabas he was a second-generation member of the first century apostolic teams, and worked in Corinth in tandem with Paul (1 Corinthians 3:6). The letter's author, if not Paul, was clearly familiar with Pauline themes.

3) A woman such as Priscilla wrote it. This is unlikely because the author fails to note any of the many great women of faith, other than Abraham's wife Sarah and Rahab, in chapter 11. On the contrary, Barak is noted rather than the true heroine of

---

[xlii] Galatians 1:11-12: 'The gospel which was preached by me is not according to man. For I neither received it from man, nor was I taught it, but I received it through a revelation of Jesus Christ.'

[xliii] 1 Corinthians 15:8: 'Last of all, as to one untimely born, he appeared to me also.'

Judges chapter 4 who is Deborah, and the unlikely Jephthah is also mentioned, whose rash vow led to him sacrificing his only daughter. These men stand in stark contrast to the great women of faith such as Ruth, Hannah and Jael whose lives the Scripture celebrates.

4) Barnabas wrote it. Barnabas served with Paul and was a friend of Timothy. The Church father Tertullian [52] wrote ('On Modesty', chapter 2): 'For there is extant withal an Epistle to the Hebrews under the name of Barnabas - a man sufficiently accredited by God, as being one whom Paul has stationed next to himself in the uninterrupted observance of abstinence.' Barnabas spoke second to Paul in Lystra (Acts 14:12), however this may be simply because Paul was senior to him, and so did more of the public speaking. Barnabas was from Cyprus, hence likely to be familiar with the Septuagint (Greek) version of the Jewish scriptures. He was also a Levite (Acts 4:36), and was cousin to John Mark, whose family were residents of Jerusalem (Acts 12:12), hence likely to have been familiar with both the Hebrew scrolls and the Greek versions.

The early Church chronicler Eusebius of Caesarea [53] quotes the Church father Origen [54] as saying that 'Who wrote the epistle, in truth, God knows.' Origen acknowledges the influence of Pauline themes, but adds, 'If I gave my opinion, I should say that the thoughts are those of the apostle, but the diction and phraseology are those of someone who remembered the apostolic teachings, and wrote down at his leisure what had been said by his teacher.' [55]

Given Tertullian's comment on authorship the opinion of this author is that Barnabas is the main contender to have composed the book having been a ministry partner of Paul.

The question of dating is primarily one of whether the book was written before or after the fall of Jerusalem in AD 70. The writer makes no allusion whatsoever to this devastation, which he would have been extremely likely to have done given his points about Jesus' sacrifice having superseded the priests' sacrifices. Instead he writes about the sacrificial priestly services in the present tense, i.e. they were still taking place. Timothy is still alive (he is believed to have died in Ephesus in 80 AD).

The writer sends the greetings of 'Those from Italy'. These are likely to be the Jewish believers in Christ who were expelled from Rome with the rest of the Jews by Emperor Claudius in 49 AD ('Claudius had commanded all the Jews to leave Rome' - Acts 18:2), and also recorded by the Roman historian Suetonius [56] in his work 'The Life of Claudius'. Emperor Nero allowed Jews to return in 54AD (though not all did); the warnings against apostasy that the Book of Hebrews emphasises may therefore date the book nearer to the persecutions that the fire of Rome precipitated in 64AD. The writer's audience had 'not yet resisted to the point of shedding their blood' (Hebrews 12:4), hence it is likely that the violent persecutions under Emperor Nero (64AD) had yet to commence.

References

[1] Strong's Greek and Hebrew Dictionary

[2] Vine's Expository Dictionary

[3] The Mishnah, Sanhedrin iii 3, Gemara 25a, b

[4] Acts 18:3 'Because he was of the same trade, he stayed with them and they were working, for by trade they were tent-makers.'

[5] 'The Jesus Discovery', Dr A T Bradford, Templehouse Publishing, ISBN 9780956479808

[6] Strong's Greek and Hebrew Dictionary

[7] Vine's Expository Dictionary

[8] Strong's Greek and Hebrew Dictionary

[9] Strong's Greek and Hebrew Dictionary

[10] 'The Jesus Discovery', Dr A T Bradford, Templehouse Publishing, ISBN 9780956479808

[11] Vine's Expository Dictionary

[12] Vine's Expository Dictionary

[13] Vine's Expository Dictionary

[14] Vine's Expository Dictionary

[15] Strong's Greek and Hebrew Dictionary

[16] Strong's Greek and Hebrew Dictionary

[17] 'All ye who have washed, come and cast lots' (Mishnah, Tamid. i. 1, 2).

[18] Mishnah Shekalim 8:5

[19] Luke 1:5 and 1:36

[20] Josephus' 'Antiquities' book 15, chapter 11

[21] Strong's Greek and Hebrew Dictionary

[22] Strong's Greek and Hebrew Dictionary

[23] 'The Temple - Its Ministry and Services' Alfred Edersheim

[24] 'The Temple - Its Ministry and Services' Alfred Edersheim

[25] 'The Temple - Its Ministry and Services' Alfred Edersheim

[26] Strong's Greek and Hebrew Dictionary

[27] Cyril of Alexandria (c. 376 - 444)

[28] Josephus' 'Antiquities' book 15, chapter 11

[29] Strong's Greek and Hebrew Dictionary

[30] Vine's Expository Dictionary

[31] 'The Temple - Its Ministry and Services' Alfred Edersheim

[32] Adam Clarke 'The New Testament of our Lord and Saviour Jesus Christ'

[33] See 'The Absence of Sacrifices and Offerings in the Life of Christ', 'The Jesus Discovery', Dr A T Bradford, Templehouse Publishing, ISBN 9780956479808

[34] Mishnah Shekalim 8, 5

[35] Barnabas Fund, 9 Priory Row, Coventry, CV1 5EX. info@barnabasfund.org

[36] Strong's Greek and Hebrew Dictionary

[37] 'The Jesus Discovery', Dr A T Bradford, Templehouse Publishing, ISBN 9780956479808

[38] Mishnah Tractate Avot 5:21

[39] Strong's Greek and Hebrew Dictionary

[40] Strong's Greek and Hebrew Dictionary

[41] Strong's Greek and Hebrew Dictionary

[42] Vine's Expository Dictionary

[43] Strong's Greek and Hebrew Dictionary

[44] Strong's Greek and Hebrew Dictionary

45 NASB Greek-Hebrew Dictionary

46 Josephus' 'The Wars Of The Jews' chapter 8, 2

47 Strong's Greek and Hebrew Dictionary

48 Vine's Expository Dictionary

49 Strong's Greek and Hebrew Dictionary

50 Vine's Expository Dictionary

51 Demosthenes (384 - 322 BC) was a prominent legal orator and politician in ancient Athens.

52 Quintus Septimius Florens Tertullianus, otherwise known as Tertullian (c. 150 – c. 220 AD), an early Christian writer born in Carthage in Africa

53 Eusebius (c. 263 - 339 AD) was Bishop of Caesarea Maritima.

54 Origen Adamantius, (c. 184 - 253 AD), an Alexandrian Church father

55 Eusebius' 'Life of Constantine', Chapter 25

56 Gaius Suetonius Tranquillus, (c. 69 - 130 AD)

Also By This Author:

'The Jesus Discovery - Another Look at Christ's Missing Years' ISBN 9780956479808. A Roman historical basis for the life of Joseph as a trainer of the priests who built Herod's Temple, together with Jewish Law informing the reaction of the Doctors who met Jesus aged 12, show Jesus to be a senior ordained Torah scholar and from a significant family in first century Judea.

'According To Matthew - A Commentary On Matthew's Gospel' ISBN 9780956479839. A verse-by-verse commentary on Matthew's Gospel revealing the Jewish Jesus as recorded by a Jew, for Jews.

'The New Testament On Women - What Every Man Should Know' ISBN 9780956479815. An analysis of every verse concerning the status of women in the New Testament, showing the Apostles' teaching to faithfully mirror Jesus' teaching of equality in status.

'El Descubrimiento de Jesús, Otra Mirada a los Años Perdidos de Cristo' (Spanish Edition of 'The Jesus Discovery') ISBN 9780956479846

'Out Of The Dark Woods. Dylan, Depression and Faith - The Messages Behind The Music Of Bob Dylan.' ISBN 9780956479822 Revealing the many biblical references in the post-1981 songs of Bob Dylan, together with evidence of a previously unrecognised depressive illness in the lyrics of 'Time Out Of Mind'.

www.ingramcontent.com/pod-product-compliance
Lightning Source LLC
Chambersburg PA
CBHW072335300426
44109CB00042B/1626